PROGRESS IN WRITING

J. W. Walter
April, 1973
Urbana

PROGRESS IN WRITING
A Learning Program

James A. Gowen

Professor of English
University of Kansas

McGraw-Hill Book Company

New York   St. Louis   San Francisco   Düsseldorf
Johannesburg   Kuala Lumpur   London   Mexico
Montreal   New Delhi   Panama
Rio de Janeiro   Singapore   Sydney   Toronto

Library of Congress Cataloging in Publication Data

Gowen, James A.

   Progress in Writing.

   1. English language--Rhetoric--Programmed instruction.

I. Title.

PE1413.G68   808'.042   72-5905

ISBN 0-07-023859-6

Progress In Writing
A Learning Program

1234567890 DODO 798765432

This book was set in Theme by Allen-Wayne Technical Corp.
The editors were David Edwards, Harriet B. Malkin, and Susan Gamer;
the designer was Jerry Lieberman;
and the production supervisor was Thomas J. Lo Pinto.
The printer and binder was R. R. Donnelley & Sons Company.

CONTENTS

PREFACE

Typically, composition texts concentrate on grammar and usage—on analyzing sentence structures, on placing periods and commas correctly, on distinguishing between *who* and *whom.* **Progress In Writing** contains nothing whatever about such matters. As one wise teacher has said, we don't write grammar, we write English. Of course it certainly helps writing if, for instance, commas and periods are where they belong. But good writing is not the result of correctness. Rather, it is the result of effective word choice, skillful sentence building, sound paragraph organization, and finally, meaningful and coherent arrangement of all parts. The four sections of this text are directed at these four crucial aspects of writing. When the student has finished, he will know all the major decisions a writer has to make and the ways to make these decisions successfully in his own writing.

Progress in Writing is different from ordinary composition texts in another important way. It is a programmed text, in which each segment, or frame, is part of a learning sequence that begins with the simplest ideas related to a subject and progresses by short steps to the more difficult. Each frame requires a response by the student; as a result, his study must be active. At the side of each frame is the correct response so that the student can check himself at each step and thus guard against uncertainty or error. Another advantage of a text such as this is that the student works independently, proceeding at the rate that best suits his own learning needs.

Now that programmed texts are fairly common, most students know how to use them without instruction. However, to be sure that all students using the text get off to a good start, the teacher should go over with them the brief section "To the Student," which directly precedes Part One, and then help them complete the first three or four frames.

An early version of the present text was tested among several hundred students, and the results of those tests, together with the comments and criticism of those who participated, were invaluable in the modification of the text for publication. I would like to acknowledge my gratitude, therefore, to the following teachers and their students: Raymond O'Dea, Ferris State College, Big Rapids, Michigan, and Marinus Swets, Grand Rapids Junior College, Grand Rapids, Michigan.

Particularly helpful in the final revision of the text were the suggestions and criticisms kindly offered by Dr. J. William Moore, Bucknell University, and James R. Moore, Mt. San Antonio College, Walnut, California.

James A. Gowen

TO THE STUDENT

Before beginning **Progress in Writing**, glance through the text briefly. Notice that it is divided into short units, each one marked by a small box at the end: □. These units, called "frames," give information and require a response of some kind such as filling in a blank or choosing between alternative words. Directly beside each frame is the correct response.

When you begin the text, cover the response column at the side of the page with a folded piece of paper. Read the frame and complete the response required by filling in the blank or marking the correct choice. Don't guess. If you have read the frame carefully, you will know the correct response. Then check to see that your response is right. If it is, go on to the next frame. If it is not, reread the frame to find out where you went wrong, correct your response, and then go on to the next frame.

Be sure to cover the response column before beginning each frame and to uncover it only after you have completed your response. Your eyes will always tend to wander when you are thinking, even when you try to keep them from doing so, and obviously just copying the correct response is not going to help you learn much. The correct responses are printed beside the frames only to protect you against the possibility of taking a false step in the learning process.

Briefly, then, here are the directions:

Cover the response column.

Read the frame and complete it.

Check your response.

Correct any error before continuing.

This book is designed the way it is for only one purpose—to help you make your writing easier and better. Give it a chance to do so by following the instructions carefully.

James A. Gowen

PROGRESS IN WRITING

ONE
WORDS

Words are the building blocks of writing. When we speak or write, we try to use the words that suit our purpose best—to explain or describe something, to tell a story, or just to express our feelings. In Part One we will be looking at the various kinds of words there are and the various ways we choose words to make our writing clear and effective.

DENOTATION AND CONNOTATION

Choosing words to fit the exact meaning we have in mind takes some care, as this example shows:

This perfume has a lovely stench.

The word very much out of place in this sentence is

_____. ☐

stench

Without referring to a dictionary, we know that *stench* has the basic meaning of smell. But that's only part of its meaning. In addition, it means a smell that is (pleasant, unpleasant). ☐

unpleasant

This perfume has a lovely fragrance.

Now the sentence is right because *fragrance* means a smell that is (pleasant, unpleasant). ☐

pleasant

It's not enough, then, to consider only a word's basic meaning. *Stench* and *fragrance* have the same basic meaning but aren't interchangeable.

> *She's thrifty.*

> *He's cheap.*

Both *thrifty* and *cheap* have the same basic meaning, a tendency to avoid spending, but their total meanings are (the same, *different* | different). ☐

denote | The basic meaning of a word is called "denotation." *Stench* and *fragrance* denote smell. *Thrifty* and *cheap* _____ a tendency to avoid spending. ☐

The difference between *stench* and *fragrance*, or *thrifty* and *cheap*, is not the denotation but rather the feelings we have about them. *Stench* and *cheap* suggest unpleasant feelings; *fragrance* and *pleasant* | *thrifty* suggest (pleasant, unpleasant) feelings. ☐

> *I am firm.*

> *You are stubborn.*

Firm and *stubborn* both denote an unbending quality, but the feelings each word suggests are different. *Firm* suggests something *good   bad* | (good, bad), whereas *stubborn* suggests something (good, bad). ☐

The feelings a word suggests are part of its meaning. We call this part the "connotation." *Firm* connotes something good; *connotes* | *stubborn* _____ something bad. ☐

Meaning, then, has two parts. Denotation is the idea a word carries; connotation is the feelings a word suggests.

> *She's very slender.*

> *She's very skinny.*

Both *slender* and *skinny* denote thin. But *slender* connotes some- *good   bad* | thing (good, bad), and *skinny* connotes something (good, bad). ☐

This dress is loud.

This dress is colorful.

Both *loud* and *colorful* (denote, connote) bright color, but *loud* (denotes, connotes) something unfavorable. ☐

When we talk about the idea a word conveys, we use the term (denotation, connotation). ☐

Connotation, on the other hand, is the part of meaning that has to do with the (idea, feelings) a word suggests. ☐

Some words are rich in connotation. Think for a minute about all the feelings that the word *home* suggests—love, warmth, comfort, protection, and so forth. Does the word *house* have the same connotation as *home?* _____ ☐

House is one of many words in the language that suggest very little, if any, feeling. Other examples are *cement, chair, pencil.* All such words have very little, if any, (denotation, connotation). ☐

Compare with *chair* and *pencil* such words as *joy* and *pain.* Do these words suggest feelings? Yes, quite a lot. An important part of their meaning, therefore, is what they (denote, connote). ☐

Scientific and technical terms are examples of words that don't suggest feelings. *Carbon, circuit, hexagon, transistor*—these words have little, if any, (denotative, connotative) meaning. ☐

A very large number of the words we use regularly, however, do have connotations that we need to take into account.

He is an individualist.

He is peculiar.

Both *individualist* and *peculiar* refer to a person whose behavior is different or unusual. But only one word suggests a favorable feeling, _____. ☐

denote
connotes
denotation
feelings
no
connotation
connote
connotative
individualist

Individualist and *peculiar,* then, refer to the same idea but suggest

denotation | different feelings. That is, they have the same (denotation,
connotation | connotation) but a different (denotation, connotation). □

> *My father tends to be (heavyset, fat).*

Suppose *father* here refers to a person who weighed more than he
should. Both *heavyset* and *fat* have the same denotation, but only

fat | one suggests that the condition is unfavorable, *(heavyset, fat).* □

Denotation and connotation, the two dimensions of meaning, give
the writer a rich variety of choices. He can express not only ideas
but also particular feelings about those ideas. Look, for instance,
at some of the possibilities in the expression of one idea, that of
mental ability:

> cunning   brilliant
> intelligent   sharp

Two of these words suggest something favorable:

intelligent brilliant | _____ and _____ . □

Sharp and *cunning* denote mental ability, but they connote
something unfavorable. We would say *brilliant student,* for
instance, but we would not ordinarily say *cunning student.*
We might in some special meaning say *brilliant robber,* but we

cunning | would be more likely to say *(intelligent, cunning) robber.* □

Arrange the following words according to connotation, from
least to most unfavorable:

> boozer   drinker   wino

drinker boozer wino | _____ _____ _____ □

least   more   most unfavorable

A man may call himself a *peddler,* a *salesman,* or a *merchandiser.*
All three denote a person who sells something. But one has a
very favorable connotation, another a less favorable, and one an
unfavorable connotation:

merchandiser salesman peddler | _____ _____ _____ □

most   less   least favorable

To express a particular idea, then, we often have a choice among two or more words, allowing us to express the exact denotation and exact connotation we have in mind.

> The American (draft, selective service system) needs revamping, some critics say.

If we wish to convey a more favorable connotation, we will complete this sentence with *(draft, selective service system)*. □   *selective service system*

Complete the following frames as a brief review:

> An important part of a politician's education is learning how to (cooperate, connive).

If we wish to convey a less favorable connotation, we will choose *(cooperate, connive)*. □   *connive*

> As a rule, the American consumer is very (trusting, gullible) when reading or listening to advertising.

The word with the more favorable connotation for this sentence is *(trusting, gullible)*. □   *trusting*

> The candle and fire cast a very (soft, weak) light over the objects in the room.

The word that gives a more appealing impression is *(soft, weak)*. □   *soft*

> Many gourmets prefer (chilled, icy) wine with their suppers.

The more appetizing word is *(chilled, icy)*. □   *chilled*

> The student leaders called upon the president to adopt several (bold, reckless) new policies.

The more frightening word is *(bold, reckless)*. □   *reckless*

> She has a large (beauty mark, mole) on her chin.

The more attractive completion is *(beauty mark, mole)*. □   *beauty mark*

> Robert Nunly turned out to be just the kind of political (leader, figure, rabble-rouser) that some voters had feared.

The most critical word is *(leader, figure, rabble-rouser)*. □   *rabble-rouser*

ABSTRACT AND CONCRETE WORDS

All writing, no matter what its purpose is, should be so clear that the reader can understand it instantly. Obviously no reader can make clear for himself something that the writer has left unclear. It is the writer's responsibility, then, to see that each of his statements means just what he wants it to mean.

Clarity is the result partly of successful word choice. And one problem in choosing the best word for each purpose is deciding how concrete the word should be.

1. *He parked his transportation in the driveway.*
2. *He parked his car in the driveway.*

Which of these sentences seems clearer? For now, don't worry about why. Sentence _____ □

2

Saying *He parked his transportation in the driveway* might be good for a laugh, but unless we know what *transportation* refers to, we can't really understand the sentence. Yet there's nothing seriously wrong with *transportation* here because a car (is, is not) a means of transportation. □

is

Can *transportation* also refer to *motorcycle, truck, sailboat,* or *dogsled?* (yes, no) □

yes

We say that *transportation* is more abstract than *car* or *dogsled* because it can refer to more things. Similarly, *tool* is (more, less), abstract than *hammer* or *scissors* because it can refer to more things. □

more

We say that the more specific words like *car* and *hammer* are more concrete. Of the words *fruit* and *apple, fruit* is more (abstract, concrete), and *apple* is more (abstract, concrete). □

abstract

concrete

Here's a good way to tell how concrete a word is: try to form a mental picture from it. If you can do so fairly easily, the word is concrete. For instance, which of these words allows you to form a mental picture more easily, *animal* or *elephant?*

_____ ☐

elephant

With the word *elephant,* you can visualize the animal's large size, the trunk, the tusks, the floppy ears, and so forth. With the word *animal,* you can visualize very little, if anything at all. *Elephant,* then, is more (concrete, abstract) than *animal.* ☐

concrete

The harder it is to form a mental picture from a word, the more abstract that word is. Which is more abstract, *thing* or *button?*

_____ ☐

thing

Remember the mental picture test. *Chair* and *table* are more (concrete, abstract) than *furniture.* ☐

concrete

It's difficult to form mental pictures from abstract words because they refer to more things than concrete words do. The word *furniture* includes the ideas of *chair* and *table* as well as many others—*lamp, stool, buffet,* and so forth. Similarly, the abstract word *container* includes the ideas of *jar, bottle,* and *bucket.* Can you name three others? _____ _____

_____ ☐

Can, bowl, barrel, tank are a few you might have listed.

It's easier to form a mental picture from a concrete word because it refers to fewer things. Which of the following refers to fewer things, *machine* or *typewriter?* _____ ☐

typewriter

A typewriter we can easily visualize, but there are so many kinds of machines that forming a mental picture from just the word *machine* is almost impossible. *Machine,* then, is much more (concrete, abstract) than *typewriter.* ☐

abstract

Remember, concrete words are easier to visualize because they refer to fewer things. In each of the following pairs, pick the word that is more concrete:

vegetable   *oak*   *dictionary*

carrot oak dictionary   *carrot*   *tree*   *book*   □

Abstract words are harder to visualize because they refer to more things. This time, pick the more abstract words in these pairs:

picture   *Boeing 747*   *wood*

picture airplane material   *painting*   *airplane*   *material* □

So far we have been looking at words in pairs, one abstract and one concrete. But words are not just abstract or concrete.

material   *wood*   *pine*

As we have already seen, *wood* is more concrete than *material*, but *pine* is (more, less) concrete than *wood* because it refers to one kind of wood. □

more

clothing   *sweater*   *cardigan*

Reading from left to right, each word here is less (abstract, concrete) than the one before. □

abstract

( ) *house*   ( ) *building*   ( ) *split-level*

Number these three words, from the most abstract (1) to the most concrete (3). □

(1) building (2) house
(3) split-level

Here's how it works: a house is a kind of building and a split-level is a kind of _____ . □

house

( ) *iodine*   ( ) *thing*   ( ) *poison*

Number these three words from most abstract to most concrete. □

(1) thing (2) poison (3) iodine

( ) *girl*   ( ) *person*   ( ) *being*   ( ) *Shirley*

Do the same with these four words. □

(1) being (2) person (3) girl
(4) Shirley

What good is knowing how abstract a word is? To answer that question, let's go back to an example we have already looked at.

He parked his transportation in the driveway.

He parked his car in the driveway.

Remember, we said that the clearer sentence is the (first, second). □

second

The second sentence is clearer because *car* replaces *transportation*. Now *car* is (more, less) concrete than *transportation*. □

more

We know that *car* is more concrete than *transportation* because it refers to fewer things and because we can form a mental picture from it (more, less) easily. □

more

As a general rule, the more concrete a word is, the clearer it is.

On the desk rested a large (thing, Bible, book).

This sentence will be really clear if completed with the most concrete word,_____. □

Bible

A vehicle swerved off the road.

In this sentence, one word is too abstract for real clarity,_____. □

vehicle

Vehicle could mean *car, motorcycle, truck,* or *bus,* and we have difficulty forming a mental picture from it.

The fisherman cut his finger on a sharp utensil.

This sentence also contains a word that is too abstract,_____. □

utensil

Fishermen use a lot of utensils—knives, hooks, jigs, scalers. Which of these did the fisherman cut his finger on? We don't know.

A _____ swerved off the road.

The fisherman cut his finger on a sharp _____.

Complete both these sentences with a concrete word. □

Any completion is correct if it is at least as concrete as *car* or *knife.*

A wealthy person owned an expensive structure.

This sentence contains two words which are too abstract,

person structure _____ *and* _____ . ☐

Person is very abstract. Two of the many more concrete words that could take its place are *man* and *lawyer*. Of those two, the

lawyer more concrete and therefore clearer word is *(man, lawyer)*. ☐

Structure also is very abstract. Of two possible substitutions, *home* and *building*, the more concrete and clearer is *(home,*

home *building)*. ☐

Because abstract words are less clear, it might seem that they're useless, to be avoided every time. Not so.

> *Barbara passed a bowl of mixed nuts.*
> *Barbara passed a bowl of mixed cashews, almonds, Brazil nuts, and peanuts.*

The second sentence is obviously more concrete and hence clearer than the first. But the first sentence does have one advantage

shorter over the second: it is _____ than the second. ☐

Abstract words allow us to economize on the number of words we need. Complete the second sentence here with one word:

> *Allen picked up a copy of* Playboy, Harper's, *and* Mad Comics.

magazines *Allen picked up three* _____ . ☐

Magazines is more abstract than *Playboy, Harper's,* and *Mad Comics.* Thus, the abstract word allows us to economize—to save words. Complete the second sentence with one word:

> *The room was filled with twenty-four women, twenty-two men, fourteen adolescent boys and girls, and twelve younger children.*

people *The room was filled with* _____ . ☐

Abstract words are economizers for the very reason that they are less clear than concrete words: they can refer to more things. For instance, more and more people are learning the usefulness of the word *sibling,* which means both brother and sister. *Sibling* is a fairly new word in the language, but we have many other, more familiar economizers. Instead of saying *father and mother,* we can substitute the familiar one-word equivalent,

_____. □   *parents*

We can say *Bananas, peaches, pears, apricots, plums, and grapes are good for you* or we can say, much more economically,

_____ *is good for you.* □   *Fruit*

Parents, siblings, and *fruit,* compared with *father, sister,* and *peach,* are more (abstract, concrete). □   *abstract*

The choice between abstract and concrete words is often a choice between clarity and economy.

> *Last Sunday I took a cab to Los Angeles International Airport and boarded a TWA 747 for John F. Kennedy International Airport, where I took a limousine to downtown New York City.*

If all these details are necessary, the writer should include them. But if they're not, he can substitute a single more abstract word:

> *Last Sunday I _____ to New York City.* □   *flew* or *went*

Often, using an abstract word in place of a concrete word is not a matter of economy.

> *He took a thing from his pocket.*
> *He took a penknife from his pocket.*

Here using the abstract word *thing* in place of the concrete word *penknife* (does, does not) allow the use of fewer words. □   *does not*

Harry went all the way home.

Harry ran all the way home.

concrete | Here's another case. The second sentence is just as short as the first, but it's clearer because *ran* is more (concrete, abstract) than *went*. ☐

A Volkswagen, four Chevrolets, two Fords, a Plymouth, and a Cadillac were involved in a minor rear-end collision today.

Nine cars were involved in a minor rear-end collision today.

economy | Here there is a real choice between using one abstract word or several concrete words. The writer must decide which he wants, clarity (the concrete words) or _____ (the abstract word). ☐

As a general rule, the more concrete a word is, the clearer it is. Stick to concrete words unless you need to economize.

A person gave the child a piece of candy.

Mrs. Rogers gave the baby Karen something.

Here are two sentences with similar meaning. Combine the sentences, using only the more concrete parts from each:

Mrs. Rogers gave the baby Karen a piece of candy.

_____

_____ ☐

Do the same with these sentences: combine them into one, using the most concrete parts from both:

The man hurt his elbow recently.

Coach Grover cut his arm this morning.

Coach Grover cut his elbow this morning.

_____

_____ ☐

Do it again with these:

Certain people enjoy unacceptable behavior.

Some children get satisfaction from breaking windows.

_____

_____ ☐

Some children enjoy breaking windows.

While we focus our attention on choosing concrete words whenever possible, let's not forget that we can economize by replacing unnecessary concrete words with a single abstract word. Complete the second sentence here with one abstract word:

The carpenter carried his hammer, power saw, and chisels with him up the ladder.

The carpenter carried his _____ with him up the ladder. ☐

tools

When economy is more important, we use the abstract word—but only when real economy is possible. The general rule stands: the more concrete your writing is, the better. Combine these sentences into one concrete sentence:

Someone replaced a fuse in the apparatus.

Mr. Scott repaired the computer.

_____

_____ ☐

Mr. Scott replaced a fuse in the computer.

Concrete suggests something solid. Give your readers something solid by choosing concrete words. Combine the following two sentences to form one solid—concrete—sentence.

Usually mankind likes floral objects.

Usually people feel positive about flowers.

_____

_____ ☐

Usually people like flowers.

Let's review now. Words are more concrete if they refer to fewer things and if it is easy to form a mental picture from them. Compared with an abstract word like *clothing,* a word like *hat* or *jacket* is _____. ☐

concrete

A word is more abstract if it can refer to more things and if it is hard or impossible to form a mental picture from it. Of the words *color* and *blue,* for instance, *color* is more (abstract, concrete). ☐

abstract

When writing, if we have a choice between an abstract word and a concrete word, the better is probably the (concrete, abstract) word. ☐

concrete

The only time we would choose an abstract word is when one abstract word can take the place of several unnecessary concrete words.

> *An Irish setter, a beagle, and a German shepherd chased the girl.*

If the concrete words are not necessary, we can substitute a single more abstract word for them:

dogs

> *Three _____ chased the girl.* ☐

To complete the review, let's combine a couple more sentence pairs. Remember, choose only the concrete elements from each.

> *A human being dashed from the area.*
> *A young boy went from the backyard.*

A young boy dashed from the

_____

backyard.

_____ ☐

One more pair:

> *In 1960, some people elected a certain Irish-Catholic their president.*
> *In 1960, the American voters indicated a preference for John F. Kennedy for the post.*

In 1960, the American voters

_____

elected John F. Kennedy

_____

their president.

_____ ☐

CLICHÉS

Some people's prose looks as though they've written it with rubber stamps. *Sharp as a tack, far be it from me, the long arm of the law*—these are examples of phrases that some writers use without being aware that they're worn out from so much use. These rubber stamps are called "clichés" (klee-SHAYZ). When we come across them, we know that the writer has simply reached into a drawer and, without thinking, pulled out a stamp that vaguely fitted his purpose. The effect of such secondhand writing is that it tunes the reader completely out. Why should anyone think about what someone else has written if the writer himself hasn't thought carefully about it?

Clichés, then, are a sure sign of careless writing. But they're easily avoided because they're easily recognized. For instance, you can complete the cliché in this sentence without even thinking:

> *We have been asked to lend a helping _____.* □

hand

How about these?

> *The whole team breathed a _____ of relief.*

sigh

> *The work was going forward by leaps and _____.* □

bounds

Clichés are recognizable for precisely the reason they're so often used: they've been around for a long time. Underline the three clichés in this sentence:

> *After working like a dog, he was tired but happy and hungry as a bear.* □

working like a dog

tired but happy hungry as a bear

Complete the clichés in this sentence:

> *His accident was just one of those _____, but that's the way it _____.* □

things

goes

Complete these:

sweet

suspicion

head

The meeting was short but _____, and we all had the sneaking _____ that Mr. Day was just talking off the top of his _____. ☐

Once upon a time, of course, clichés were not clichés. They were fresh, powerful expressions of the world's greatest writers. The Bible and the plays of Shakespeare are sources of many phrases which have been made into rubber stamps: *sadder but wiser, the wages of sin, the blind leading the blind.* Here are two from the Bible; see if you can complete them: *Kill the fatted*

calf   willing

weak

_____; the spirit is _____, but the flesh is _____. ☐

Occasionally, clichés can be twisted for comic effect. James Thurber twisted the cliché *Don't leave a stone unturned* to read *Don't leave a tern unstoned* in a humorous story of his. Another common twist, almost a cliché itself, is *one swell foop,* which

swoop

originally was the cliché *one fell _____.* ☐

last but not least

Least but not last is a comically twisted version of the cliché _____. ☐

hand

The humorous *He gave him the back of his tongue* is a combination of two clichés: *He gave him a tongue-lashing* and *He gave him the back of his _____.* ☐

The best rule to follow as you write is, if you've heard a particular phrase before, the chances are that it's a cliché. Unless you're sure it's not a cliché, don't use it.

In preparation for his test, he burned the midnight oil.

In preparation for his test, he studied until after midnight.

first (burned the midnight oil)

One of these sentences is built upon a cliché, the (first, second). ☐

Remember, clichés are rubber stamps, a sign of thoughtless writing.

The idea came to Edison like a bolt out of the blue.

The idea came to Edison with jarring speed.

One of these sentences is a rubber-stamp job, the (first, second). ☐   *first (bolt out of the blue)*

Develop the ability to spot a cliché as part of your writing skill so that you can edit out any that might accidentally appear in your own prose. Underline the clichés here:

In the last analysis, she was green with envy because she heard   *In the last analysis*

that a good time was had by all at the party. ☐   *green with envy*

    a good time was had by all

Even if you like the sound of a particular cliché, the chances are that your readers won't. Therefore, though your own phrases may not seem as striking or as colorful, learn to prefer an original phrase rather than a cliché. Writing cannot be improved with clichés.

The homecoming queen was unusually lovely.

The homecoming queen was as pretty as a picture.

The preferable phrasing is in the (first, second) sentence here. ☐   *first*

Henry is going to become a doctor and follow in his father's footsteps.

Henry is going to become a doctor like his father.

The preferable phrasing is in the (first, second) sentence. ☐   *second*

If you've heard it before, it's very likely a cliché.

General Lee was at the end of his rope.

General Lee was near to defeat.

General Lee had his back to the wall.

Only one of these sentences is not built on a cliché, the (first, second, third). ☐   *second*

Television keeps us abreast of the times.

Television keeps us fairly well informed.

Television provides regular news coverage.

Only one of these sentences contains a cliché, the (first, second, third). □

first (abreast of the times)

By now you should be pretty good at spotting clichés. In the list below, mark all the clichés you find:

1. *wee small hours*
2. *a hot desert*
3. *blushing bride*
4. *all work and no play*
5. *four strong men*
6. *a cheap thrill* □

1, 3, 4, 6

Remember, clichés are phrases you—and almost everyone else— have heard before. Mark the clichés here:

1. *rotten to the core*
2. *wild-goose chase*
3. *cool as a cucumber*
4. *it's a small world*
5. *the jaws of death*
6. *to make a long story short* □

They're all clichés.

FANCY LANGUAGE

One common kind of error that inexperienced writers make stems from the mistaken idea that writing well means using big words. This idea probably comes from the fact that we are more likely to find unfamiliar words in our reading than in conversations. We may then assume that writing calls for a fancier vocabulary than speaking. Also—let's be honest—we're often impressed by big or unfamiliar words, and writing gives us the chance to impress others by using such words ourselves. But when we use fancy language, we can create problems.

He responded in the affirmative.
Though fancy, this sentence is easy for most of us to put into plain English:

He said (yes, no). ☐　　　　　　　　　　　　　　　　　*yes*

But what about a sentence like this?
The peripatetic perambulated toward the umbrageous bosket.
It is English, as surprising as it may seem, but it's the kind of fancy English that no one will use if he is at all interested in making himself understood. *Peripatetic* means walker; *perambulate* means to stroll; *umbrageous* means shady; and *bosket* means grove. Now you can put the same idea into plain English:

_____　*The walker strolled toward*

_____ ☐　*the shady grove.*

What's wrong with words like *umbrageous* and *peripatetic?* Nothing, really. They're perfectly good, healthy English words. The only trouble with using them is that most English-speaking people don't understand them.

He adumbrated the group's eleemosynary activities.
Underline the unfamiliar words here that make this sentence impossible for most people to understand. ☐　　*adumbrated   eleemosynary*

When we write, clarity is our first consideration. And fancy language can obscure meaning.

He adumbrated the group's eleemosynary activities.

He outlined the group's charitable works.

Both these sentences have the same meaning. Obviously the clearer one is the one composed of (simple, fancy) language. ☐

simple

A reader impressed by big words won't understand them, and a reader who understands them won't be impressed. Generally speaking, then, it is wiser to choose the (more, less) familiar word when there is a choice. ☐

more

Both the following sentences mean the same thing. Combine them into one, composed entirely of the more familiar words.

That lying quidnunc said that I was culpable.

That mendacious busybody averred that I was guilty.

That lying busybody said that I was guilty.

_____

_____ ☐

Trying to impress others with big words often has quite the opposite effect. Like the little girl trying to make a muscle, we get only a laugh. Combine these sentences to make one that avoids being accidentally funny. If you don't find it helpful to write out the entire sentence, just underline the parts you choose, making sure they add up to a complete sentence.

He indited a long epistle to George.

He wrote a prolix letter to George.

He wrote a long letter to George.

_____

_____ ☐

There's nothing wrong with unfamiliar words. The more we know, the better we can read because we do run across such words occasionally. But it's a good idea to avoid them in our writing—unless we have a very good reason for using them. Combine the following sentences to avoid all less familiar words:

The holistic rule is to eschew long words when limning.

The general theorem is to avoid sesquipedalian words when writing.

_____

_____ □

The general rule is to avoid long words when writing.

The only reason for using a word unfamiliar to our readers is that the word has no familiar substitute, a situation that rarely happens except in technical matters. You'll improve your writing in almost every case by using the simpler, more familiar word. Combine these sentences accordingly:

Looking at the star traceries in the firmament can make me dizzy.

Looking at the sidereal patterns in the sky can make me vertiginous.

_____

_____ □

Looking at the star patterns in the sky can make me dizzy.

So far we've talked about fancy language as though it meant only unfamiliar words. There is more to it than just that, however.

I live on Elm Street.

I reside on Elm Street.

Neither *live* nor *reside* is unfamiliar, but one has definitely a fancier sound, *(live, reside).* □

reside

The chemist terminated the experiment.

The chemist ended the experiment.

terminated | Of the two, the fancier word is *(terminated, ended).* □

Words like *reside* and *terminate* belong to a large family of words that are familiar but sound a bit too fancy for everyday use. Such words are easily recognized. For instance, even though not in a sentence, the fancier of the words *procrastinate* and

procrastinate | *delay* is _____ . □

veracity | Of *truth* and *veracity*, the fancier word is _____ . □

What happens when we use words like *procrastinate, reside, terminate,* and *veracity?* We can expect almost all our readers to understand us, of course. But we're putting a kind of distance between ourselves and our readers and suggesting at the same time that our ideas are more important than those of other people. In short, we're putting on airs, talking down to others. Underline the one word in the following sentence that suggests the writer has put on special airs:

The four chairmen agreed that the meeting commenced

commenced | *promptly at eight.* □

There is a perfectly respectable substitute for *commenced.* Insert it here.

The four chairmen agreed that the meeting _____

began | *promptly at eight.* □

I will leave for Florida tomorrow.

I will depart for Florida tomorrow.

We would be justified in feeling that the writer of the (first,

second | second) sentence was talking down to us just a little bit. □

Mr. Elkins relinquished his employment.

Mr. Elkins quit his job.

The writer of one of these sentences is putting on considerable

first | airs, the (first, second) sentence. □

Like unfamiliar words, fancy though familiar language can have the effect of accidental humor. Combine these sentences in one to avoid that possibility:

Marianne was betrothed six months before her wedding.

Marianne was engaged six months before her nuptials.

_____

_____ □

Marianne was engaged six months before her wedding.

Fancy language seems to appear regularly in political speeches and official statements from governmental agencies and businesses. Sometimes the fancy language is an attempt to cover up the fact that the person has nothing—or very little—to say.

Doctors concur that Americans tend to be too corpulent for a salutary life.

Doctors agree that Americans tend to be too fat for a healthy life.

The obvious fact that being overweight is unhealthy sounds much more profound when expressed in the fancy language of the (first, second) sentence. □

first

The East Coast cities lost all electrical power for five minutes.

The Eastern Seaboard metropolitan areas experienced a total electrical power outage for a five-minute period.

Which sentence is more likely an official statement meant to sound important? (the first, the second) □

the second

Let's have a little fun and combine the following sentences into one that is as fancy as possible. As you will see, the result will be a comically pompous sentence, just the kind you want to avoid in your own writing.

The president is endeavoring to increase the utility of extra functionaries.

The president is trying to maximize the use of supernumerary workers.

_____

_____

_____ □

The president is endeavoring to maximize the utility of super-numerary functionaries.

So that what you've just done won't become a bad habit, complete these sentences to make one that is as simple and direct as possible:

Please extinguish all lights before leaving the premises.

Please turn off all illuminators before quitting the room.

Please turn off all lights before leaving the room.

_____

_____ □

Occasionally, as in a formal speech, fancy language might not sound too far out of character. Most often, however, especially in writing, such language sounds stilted, fake. Combine these sentences to avoid that possibility:

The merchandiser was cognizant of the change.

The salesman knew about the alteration.

The salesman knew about the change.

_____

_____ □

Whenever you have a choice, pick the simplest word you can. In the following sentence, choose the less stilted word for each position:

president   guess
goal   enemy's
offer
explanation

The (chief of state, president) would not (guess, conjecture) about the (desideratum, goal) of his (adversary's, enemy's) program, nor would he (offer, tender) any (elucidation, explanation) of his own. □

SLANG

At the other extreme from fancy language is slang. Now let's understand from the beginning that there's nothing wrong with slang. In fact, in certain situations there is everything right about it. But slang, particularly in writing, creates problems we had better face squarely.

First of all, what is slang? The term *slang*, strictly speaking, refers to expressions not considered part of standard English, expressions we use only in informal conversations with friends.

> *Let's leave.*
> *Let's split.*

Only one of these expressions is truly informal, the (first, second). ☐

second

Since *split* with the meaning of *leave* is seldom used except in informal conversations, we call it slang.

> *That guy is really square.*

This sentence has two slang expressions. Underline them. ☐

guy   square

How do we recognize slang? Since slang is more at home in informal conversations than in writing, it's fairly easy to recognize. Which are we more likely to hear in conversations than see written, *make a mistake* or *goof?* _____ ☐

goof

Identify the slang expressions in each of the following pairs:

> *pad   girl   television*
> *apartment   chick   boob tube* ☐

pad   chick   boob tube

Slang, then, tends always to be part of spoken rather than written English.

> *Some politicians expect people to believe that garbage.*
> *Some politicians expect people to believe those lies.*

We are more likely to hear one of these sentences spoken than to see it written, the (first, second). ☐

first

One big problem in using slang in our writing is that not everyone understands slang expressions.

lounge lizard

flake out

nosy

You probably recognize only
the last, *nosy*.

Which of these slang expressions do you recognize? ☐

Slang expressions come and go, often quickly, before many people learn their meaning. For instance, *flake out,* which meant go to bed, was popular slang twenty years ago. No one uses it now.

She's the cat's pajamas.

Probably not. The expression
cat's pajamas is about fifty
years out of date now.

Does this sentence make sense to you? _____ ☐

Not only does slang go out of date. It's often a private language— or at least semiprivate—understood only by an in-group such as musicians, surfers, or hot-rod enthusiasts. For example, a musician calls a job a *gig.* A surfer calls a particular kind of heavy surfboard a *gun.* Teen-agers have a lively slang most young people know. In the sentence *It was a cool party, cool* means (very good,

very good

very bad). ☐

As lively and as colorful as some slang expressions are, they can become pretty tiresome after we've heard them a hundred times. Like popular songs we enjoy, we can hear them too often.

The new humanities building has a far-out design.

This sentence has a slang expression that's now almost worn out,

far-out

_____ . ☐

Slang goes out of style, often very quickly; and slang is usually spoken only by an in-group. For these two reasons, slang is not as useful in our writing as the more widely understood and more permanent expressions.

She's really uptight about her studies.

She's really anxious about her studies.

Because it contains no slang, the sentence that will be understood by most people and for a longer time is the (first, second). ☐

second

Combine the following sentences into one having no slang expressions:

Trying to rap with that bore is a real drag.

Trying to talk with that nerd is very difficult.

_____

_____ ☐

Trying to talk with that bore is very difficult.

Combine these the same way:

Those old W. C. Fields flicks are really enjoyable.

Those old W. C. Fields movies really blow your mind.

_____

_____ ☐

Those old W. C. Fields movies are really enjoyable.

Occasionally, of course, we do use slang in our writing. For example, if we write a letter to a close friend, we probably (would, would not) use some slang. ☐

would

On the other hand, if we were writing a letter to the editor of a city newspaper expressing our views on, say, the poverty program, we probably (would, would not) avoid using slang. ☐

would

In writing, then, whether or not we use slang depends on who our audience is. Combine the following sentences into one that could be understood by a group of city businessmen:

Some motorists think hassling cyclists is exciting fun.
Some motorists think bothering cyclists is a groove and a gas.

Some motorists think bothering cyclists is exciting fun.

_____

_____ □

Slang, when understood and shared, can give an easy informality to our writing. Combine the following sentences into one that would be right for an informal article in the sports section of a college newspaper:

The real buffs were put off by their team's lack of effort.
The real fans were angry at their team's lack of hustle.

The real buffs were put off by their team's lack of hustle.

_____

_____ □

When we are writing for a general audience, the chances are that some readers may not understand or share our slang. Rewrite these sentences as one that would be suitable for such an audience:

The hash they serve at some frats is really terrible.
The food they sling at some fraternity houses is real slop.

The food they serve at some fraternity houses is really terrible.

_____

_____

_____ □

Combine these sentences into one for a general audience:

After the blast the men all crashed at a friend's apartment.
After the party the guys all slept at a friend's pad.

After the party the men all slept at a friend's apartment.

_____

_____ □

Now combine the same sentences into one that would be right for those who share the same slang.

_____

_____ □

After the blast the guys all crashed at a friend's pad.

Slang, then, though right for very informal situations in conversations or writing, may be misunderstood and gets stale very quickly. When in doubt, avoid using it. Combine these sentences to avoid all slang:

　Jocks are sometimes very studious.
　Athletes are sometimes real grinds.

_____

_____ □

Athletes are sometimes very studious.

Don't be afraid of slang. When it's new, it is lively and colorful, and it can give your informal writing an easy, natural quality. But develop your sense of when to use it, when to avoid it. Combine these sentences to avoid all slang:

　My old lady really got angry when she dug my new clothes.
　My mother really blew her top when she saw my new threads.

_____

_____ □

My mother really got angry when she saw my new clothes.

JARGON

The term *jargon* has two meanings. It means, first, the special language of a particular occupation or interest. When speaking with one another, doctors, football fans, truck drivers, or accountants, for instance, use a special set of technical terms that outsiders may not understand. The second meaning of *jargon* is gobbledygook—fancy, scientific-sounding language that has little, if any meaning.

Let's talk about these two meanings of *jargon* one at a time. First, let's look at jargon as technical language.

Most people, of course, understand some of the jargon of some of the professions or interests. People other than avid sports fans would be likely to know that the terms *base hit*, *fastball*, and *shortstop* are terms related to (football, hockey, baseball). □

baseball

The terms *biopsy*, *ventricular fibrillation*, and *alveoli*, however, are not at all generally known. They are terms doctors understand and use regularly. What about the terms *lens*, *shutter*, *emulsion*, and *parallax?* You probably don't know them all, but you recognize enough to know that they are terms (photographers, skiers, cyclists) use. □

photographers

The following terms are part of the jargon—the technical language—of sailing. How many do you recognize?

clew	*sextant*	*sail*
spinnaker	*lazaret*	*stern* □

Unless you are a sailor, you probably recognize only *sail, stern,* and possibly *sextant.*

You would expect that a doctor writing to an audience of doctors or a photographer writing to an audience of photographers (could, could not) use the jargon of their occupation without being misunderstood. □

could

The important word is *audience:* who is it you are writing to? And the rule is, don't use words your audience probably can't understand. Let's suppose you're a biologist trying to explain something to a group of non-biologists. Which of the following terms could you expect your audience to understand?

oxygen	*photosynthesis*	*hemoglobin*
air	*carbon dioxide*	*respiration* ☐

Probably *oxygen*, *air*, and *respiration*.

Like the fancy language we've already looked at in an earlier section, jargon may impress some people who don't understand it. But if you write to communicate rather than impress, you'll use only those technical terms you can count on your audience's knowing. Which of the following basketball terms could you expect a general audience of non-fans to understand without explanation?

dribble	*one-and-one*	*shoot*
turnover	*baseline*	*free throw* ☐

dribble, shoot, free throw

Which of these terms having to do with the law could you expect non-lawyers to understand?

tort	*jury*	*contract*
intestate	*habeas corpus*	*trial* ☐

jury, contract, trial

If you're writing for a general audience and have to use a technical term, go ahead—but explain it in terms your audience can understand.

> *The crew then rigged the spinnaker—a large balloonlike sail that flies forward from the mast.*

Here a non-sailor (could, could not) understand the technical term *spinnaker.* ☐

could

Which of the jargon terms in this sentence need explaining for a general audience?

> *To prepare his car for racing, he needed to install a tacho-meter and new spark plugs.* _____ ☐

tachometer

To prepare his car for racing, he needed to install a tacho-meter (a gauge showing the motor's revolutions per minute) and new spark plugs.

We could expect this sentence now to be understood by (only car enthusiasts, a general audience). ☐

a general audience

When writing for a specialized audience—of computer program-mers, dairy farmers, stamp collectors—we can use the technical language, or jargon, known to the audience.

Palmer's drive sliced into the rough.
Palmer's first shot drifted to his right into trees and high grass.

Only the (first, second) sentence here is intelligible to most non-golfers. ☐

second

The last examples have shown a major advantage of jargon: its economy. One technical term can often take the place of the many nontechnical words necessary to explain its meaning.

He bought a pair of crampons.
He bought a set of steel spikes that mountain climbers fit on their shoes for walking on ice.

In the second sentence, (economy, clarity) has been sacrificed. ☐

economy

We should use the appropriate technical term whenever we are reasonably sure our audience will understand it. But clarity should never be sacrificed for economy.

In Freud's terms, the id is in constant warfare with the superego.

Psychologists can readily understand this sentence, but if it is for a more general audience, the writer probably should explain two terms. Underline them. ☐

id   superego

The Packer quarterback threw two bombs and sneaked for a third touchdown.

The average football fan would have no difficulty understanding this sentence, but for those who know little about the game, the writer should clarify two words. Underline them. ☐

bombs   sneaked

Combine these sentences to make one that the non-scientist can understand. Remember, if you find it unnecessary to write out the new sentence, just underline the parts you choose.

The young meteorologists adjusted their anemometers carefully.

The young weathermen calibrated their wind-speed measuring instruments carefully.

_____

_____

_____ ☐

The young weathermen adjusted their wind-speed measuring instruments carefully.

Now combine the same sentences into a more economical one that only those familiar with the jargon will understand.

_____

_____

_____ ☐

The young meteorologists calibrated their anemometers carefully.

Combine these sentences into one that anyone not familiar with a dentist's work can understand:

The dentist's aid then used a wide scaler on the outer side of the patient's teeth.

The dentist's aide then used a wide instrument for scraping teeth clean on the buccal side of the patient's teeth.

_____

_____

_____

_____ ☐

The dentist's aide then used a wide instrument for scraping teeth clean on the outer side of the patient's teeth.

But remember what we said earlier: *jargon* refers not just to technical terms. It also refers to technical-sounding gobbledygook that is just another kind of fancy language.

> *The child has poor motor coordination.*
>
> *The child is clumsy.*

Both these sentences mean the same thing, but obviously one of them is more direct, more easily understood, the (first, second). □

second

The term *motor coordination* may be useful in highly technical talk, but it's a wretched substitute for plain English when plain English will do. And plain English will do just fine most of the time.

> *He gave the teacher negative feedback.*

Here we would guess that some plain English substitute could be found for the words _____ and _____. □

negative   feedback

The term *negative feedback* is a perfectly respectable technical term borrowed from electronics. However, if the sentence we've looked at means only *He told the teacher no,* then the jargon *negative feedback* (is, is not) a good choice. □

is not

Jargon, in the sense we are using now, refers to the overuse of technical terms where simpler, more direct language would serve.

> *The building is oriented to the east.*
>
> *The building faces east.*

These examples show the weakness of jargon. The term that leads to an awkward, wordy sentence is _____. □

oriented

Often people will use technical terms and the resulting clumsy sentences for the same reason they use fancy language: to impress.

> *The editor described his experiences well.*
>
> *The editor verbalized his experiences well.*

The sentence here which sounds as though the writer is straining to impress us is the (first, second). □

second

Described sounds ordinary; *verbalized* sounds scientific, important.

Teachers are often poorly paid.

Instructional personnel are often poorly paid.

The two-word term here that sounds scientific, important is

_____. ☐   *Instructional personnel*

Jargon like *instructional personnel* stands in the way of meaning,
we have to think twice before we realize that it means simply
teachers.

> *The repository of books on our campus is a pleasant place to
> study.*

We have to think for a while before we realize that *repository of
books* simply means_____. ☐   *library*

We live in a highly technical world, where technical language
multiplies rapidly. Electronics, psychology, the space program—
these are just three of the hundreds of sources for special
language. For instance, *countdown, staging, hold,* and *splashdown*
are common terms of the _____ program. ☐   *space*

We know from watching TV and having space experts translate
for us that a *power-down configuration* refers to the condition
of a spaceship in which all unnecessary equipment is turned off
to save precious electricity.

> *During the day the average housewife keeps her home in a
> power-down configuration.*

The jargon expression (is, is not) out of place here. ☐   *is*

Though impressive-sounding and perhaps useful, such jargon
expressions are out of place except in the most highly technical
circles.

> *Data acquisition is often difficult.*

> *Getting information is often difficult.*

Because it avoids the heavy-handedness of jargon, the (first,
second) sentence is the better one. ☐   *second*

Even when we are writing highly technical pieces for people who understand all the terms, it's better to use plain English wherever possible. Certainly when writing for a nontechnical audience, we must take special pains to avoid jargon. Combine the following sentences in one jargon-free sentence:

> *Urban inhabitants are in danger of cancer from hydrocarbons and other atmospheric pollutants.*
> *City dwellers are liable to carcinogenic infection from smog.*

City dwellers are in danger of cancer from smog.

_____

_____ ☐

Now combine these sentences in the same way:

> *Four technical personnel saw that the access gate to the airplane was jammed.*
> *Four mechanics verified by visual inspection that the door to the airplane was dysfunctional.*

Four mechanics saw that the door to the airplane was jammed.

_____

_____

_____ ☐

Make it a habit to choose the simple and direct word wherever possible. Do so here as you combine these sentences in one:

> *A resource person representing the field of tax accountancy will answer questions after the meeting.*
> *A tax expert will provide appropriate responses following the meeting.*

A tax expert will answer questions after the meeting.

_____

_____ ☐

REVIEW: WORDS

Here we're going to begin a short review of everything we've been doing in Part One, Words. We'll use the sentence-combining device. Rewrite each sentence pair so that you have a new sentence that fulfills the instructions given with each pair. Once again, if writing out the new sentence is not helpful, simply underline the parts from each that you choose, making sure they add up to a complete sentence.

Denotation and Connotation

The ancient couple walked slowly toward the bench.
The old couple tottered toward the bench.
Show that the couple are extremely old and weak:

_____

_____ ☐   *The ancient couple tottered toward the bench.*

Two huge guards kept the mob away from the gates.
Two big guards muscled the people away from the gates.
Show that the event was brutal and frightening:

_____

_____ ☐   *Two huge guards muscled the mob away from the gates.*

The cook then broiled the beef and moistened it with a savory sauce.
The chef then cooked the steak and topped it with a good-smelling sauce.
Make the description as appetizing as possible:

_____

_____   *The chef then broiled the steak and topped it with a savory*

_____ ☐   *sauce.*

The city commissioner did not give the Citizen's League the help they needed.

The city commissioner failed to give the Citizens' League the help they demanded.

Write a version that favors the Citizens' League:

The city commissioner failed to give the Citizens' League the help they needed.

_____

_____

_____ ☐

Abstract and Concrete Words

The merchandise was burned in yesterday's misfortune.

The clothes were damaged in the recent fire.

Write a concrete version:

The clothes were burned in yesterday's fire.

_____

_____ ☐

Some people rushed from the building when they heard the sound.

Four young men went out of the building when they heard the siren.

Write a concrete version:

Four young men rushed from the building when they heard the siren.

_____

_____

_____ ☐

The fifty-two- or fifty-three-year-old woman wearing a colorful dress stood about five feet from the doorway.

The middle-aged women wearing a red and yellow polka-dot dress stood near the doorway.

This time, write an economical version using the more abstract parts:

_____

_____

_____ ☐

The middle-aged woman wearing a colorful dress stood near the doorway.

The Smiths intended to hold the event on their own premises, inviting only their closest friends.

The Smiths intended to give the party in their own home, inviting only a select group.

Write a concrete version:

_____

_____

_____ ☐

The Smiths intended to give the party in their own home, inviting only their closest friends.

Clichés

Beyond the shadow of a doubt, such people are rare.

Undoubtedly, such people are few and far between.

Write a version free of clichés:

_____

_____ ☐

Undoubtedly, such people are rare.

In this day and age, it is hard to find a secluded vacation spot.

Nowadays it is hard to find a vacation spot off the beaten track.

Write a version free of clichés:

_____

_____ ☐

Nowadays it is hard to find a secluded vacation spot.

I suspected that George was not the kind who could tolerate the difficulties of army life and make the best of a bad bargain.

I suspected that George was not the kind who could tolerate the trials and tribulations of army life and find what good there was in it.

Write a version free of clichés:

I suspected that George was not the kind who could tolerate the difficulties of army life and find what good there was in it.

_____

_____

_____

_____ ☐

To all intents and purposes, the engagement had finally ended, and Gertrude's parents breathed a sigh of relief.

Apparently the engagement was finally over and done with, and Gertrude's parents felt greatly relieved.

Write a version free of clichés:

Apparently the engagement had finally ended, and Gertrude's parents felt greatly relieved.

_____

_____

_____ ☐

Fancy Language

The construction personnel built a temporary interdiction of sandbags across the flodded thoroughfare.

The workers erected a temporary dam of sandbags across the inundated highway.

Write a version free of fancy language:

The workers built a temporary dam of sandbags across the flooded highway.

_____

_____

_____ ☐

After the meeting, anyone having positive inclinations toward helping should communicate with Mr. Grimes.

After the convocation, any individual wishing to help should speak to Mr. Grimes.

Write a version free of fancy language:

_____

_____

_____ ☐

After the meeting, anyone wishing to help should speak to Mr. Grimes.

Four of the emporiums near the juncture of Main and Central Streets were burned in the conflagration.

Four of the stores contiguous to the corner of Main and Central Streets were incinerated in the fire.

Write a version free of fancy language:

_____

_____

_____ ☐

Four of the stores near the corner of Main and Central Streets were burned in the fire.

Many comestibles eaten diurnally by Americans have a nugatory nutritional value.

Many foods ingested daily by Americans are not very nutritious.

Write a version free of fancy language:

_____

_____

_____ ☐

Many foods eaten daily by Americans are not very nutritious.

Slang

After listening to that man give out with all that mickey mouse, I got angry.
After listening to that calt talking about such stupid ideas, I lost my cool.

Write a version without slang:

After listening to that man talking about such stupid ideas, I got angry.

_____

_____

_____ ☐

The broad they just made dean of women is really attractive.
The woman they just made dean of women is out of sight.

Write a version without slang:

The woman they just made dean of women is really attractive.

_____

_____

_____ ☐

Most people dig it when the narcotics agents bust the dealers who sell smak to children and addicts.
Most people are pleased when the narcs arrest the dealers who push heroin to kids and junkies.

This time write a version that only people who know the slang can understand:

Most people dig it when the narcs bust the dealers who push smak to kids and junkies.

_____

_____

_____ ☐

The governor really blew it when he told those hip people to leave.

The governor made a serious mistake when he told those well-informed people to get lost.

Write a version that people who may not know the slang can understand:

_____

_____

_____ ☐

The governor made a serious mistake when he told those well-informed people to leave.

Jargon

The prescription was simply aspirin with a buffering agent added.

The prescription was simply sodium acetylsalicylate with a chemical to protect the stomach.

Write a version a non-druggist can understand:

_____

_____

_____ ☐

The prescription was simply aspirin with a chemical to protect the stomach.

Just as the quartermaster turned the helm to port, another ship appeared out of the fog slightly to the rear on the side away from the wind.

Just as the steersman turned the wheel to the left, another ship appeared out of the fog abaft the lee beam.

Write a version a non-sailor can understand:

_____

_____

_____

_____

_____ ☐

Just as the steersman turned the wheel to the left, another ship appeared out of the fog slightly to the rear on the side away from the wind.

The bride wore a gown of silk and organza and a veil made out of a meshlike material.

The bride wore a gown of silk and a very thin kind of material and a tulle veil.

Write a version that those who know the names of fabrics can understand:

The bride wore a gown of silk and organza and a tulle veil.

_____

_____ ☐

Pubescent girls often report negatively about being able to make friends.

Teen-age females often complain about being unable to achieve peer-group acceptance.

Write a version free of gobbledygook:

Teen-age girls often complain about being unable to make friends.

_____

_____

_____ ☐

TWO

SENTENCES

The basic unit of expression is the sentence. By themselves, words and phrases have very little precise meaning. Only when combined in certain ways do they spring into life and take on their full quota of sense. For instance, the word *light* has a different meaning in each of these sentences:

Light the fire.
Turn off the light.
The suitcase is light.

Sense, then, comes from sentences.

FOCUS

Writing is something like taking a picture. It's hard for a reader to make sense out of carelessly formed sentences just as it is hard for a viewer to make sense from an out-of-focus picture. Experienced writers are able to bring their sentences into sharp focus, using ways you can easily learn.

We all learn how to form sentences very early in our lives. A child of only two or three can form sentences and make himself understood.

I see a flower. The flower is red.

By the time a child is four or five, he will have learned how to combine such sentences into one:

I see a _____ flower. □

red

As we grow more mature, we learn to combine the ideas of several simple sentences into one.

The books are on the table. They are history books. I have to return them to the library.

We can combine these three sentences into one:

history

on the table

I have to return the _____ books _____ _____ to the library. ☐

As a matter of fact, researchers who study such matters have discovered that the better a person is in combining sentences, the more mature he is.

The ball is red. The ball is big. The ball is mine.

This sequence, then, reflects a writer who is probably (mature,

immature

immature). ☐

The ball is red. The ball is big. The ball is mine.

A more mature writer would combine these sentences into one:

The big red ball is mine.

The big _____ ball is _____. ☐

The process of combining several sentences is called "embedding." Generally, the sentences we use consist of several simple sentences embedded into another.

The rare old vase fell.

This sentence consists of the sentence *The vase fell* and two embedded sentences:

1. *The vase is rare.*

old

2. *The vase is _____.* ☐

The sentence into which other sentences are embedded is called the "base sentence." In *The rare old vase fell*, the base sentence

The vase fell.

consists of only three words, _____. ☐

In *The green light flashed*, the sentence *The light is green* is

light flashed

embedded into the base sentence *The _____*. ☐

The new record skipped.

Here the embedded sentence is *The record is new* and the

base

_____ sentence is *The record skipped.* ☐

Notice that we often have a choice of which sentence to make the base sentence and which sentence or sentences to embed.

The car is there.

The car is mine.

These sentences can be combined in either of two ways: we can say *My car is there* or *The car _____ is _____.* □

The car there is mine.

My car is there.

The car there is mine.

Both sentences carry the same bits of information, the idea of ownership *(my, mine)* and the idea of location *(there).* But in each one, the focus is different. That is, one idea stands out above the others. Without knowing exactly why, we can tell that the focus is on the idea of location in the (first, second) sentence. □

first

The brown shoe is missing.

The missing shoe is brown.

The focus is on the color of the shoe in the (first, second) sentence. □

second

Both the sentences in the last frame come from two simple sentences:

The shoe is missing.

The shoe is brown.

In *The missing shoe is brown,* the base sentence is *The _____ _____.* □

The shoe is brown.

When we build sentences by embedding them, we focus on the base sentence.

This map is accurate.

This map is new.

To combine these sentences so that the focus is on the idea of accuracy, we would use as our base sentence the (first, second) sentence. □

first

This map is accurate.

This map is new.

Combine these sentences to focus on the idea of accuracy:

This new map is accurate.

This _____. ☐

This map is accurate.

This map is new.

Now combine them to focus on the idea of newness:

This accurate map is new.

This _____. ☐

The work is finished.

The work is really difficult.

Combine these to focus on the idea of being finished:

The really difficult work is finished.

The _____

_____. ☐

Those walls are papered.

Those walls are high.

Those walls need cleaning.

Combine these three sentences to focus on the need for cleaning:

Those high papered walls need cleaning.

Those _____

_____. ☐

Let's do a couple more just to be sure you've got the idea.

The soldiers arrived by bus.

The soldiers were young.

There were several soldiers.

Focus on the arrival by bus:

Several young soldiers arrived by bus.

Several _____

_____. ☐

The styles seemed very extreme.

They were dress styles.

They were new.

Focus on the idea of the styles' being extreme:

The new dress styles seemed very extreme.

_____

_____. ☐

RELATIVE CLAUSES

In the previous section we saw how to combine fairly simple sentences so that one idea is in focus. The principle is simple: focus is always on the idea of the base sentence; all other ideas are embedded. This one principle is all you need to know in order to build many kinds of sentences in the way that suits your purposes best. Let's look now at how we use this principle with what are called "relative clauses."

Remember, focus is always on the idea of the base sentence. It follows that if we have two base sentences, the focus will be divided equally.

    The boat cost $2,000. It sank.

Here the focus is equally on the boat's cost and the fact that it

_____. □   *sank*

The situation is almost the same if we stitch the two sentences together with *and*.

    The boat cost $2,000, and it sank.

The fact of the boat's sinking and its cost, despite the connective *and*, (do, do not) share equal focus. □   *do*

But we can combine these sentences so that just one of the ideas is in focus. We can say either *The boat that cost $2,000 sank*

or *The boat that* _____ *cost $2,000.* □   *sank*

    The boat that cost $2,000 sank.
    The boat that sank cost $2,000.

Without worrying about why, we know that the focus is on cost in the (first, second) sentence and on sinking in the (first,   *second   first*
second). □

We're using what is called a relative pronoun to embed one sentence into another. *That* is a relative pronoun.

The dress that needs shortening has a high waist.

The sentence *The dress needs shortening* is embedded into the sentence *The dress has a high waist* with the relative pronoun

that _____ . ☐

We can, of course, also embed *The dress has a high waist* into *The dress needs shortening,* using *that* the same way:

that has a high waist *The dress* _____ *needs shortening.* ☐

The umbrella that tore has been repaired.

Here we have one sentence embedded into another. The sentence *The umbrella tore* is embedded into the sentence *The umbrella*

has been repaired _____ . ☐

Sentences embedded into others with relative pronouns are called, obviously enough, "relative clauses."

The umbrella that tore has been repaired.

Here the sentence *The umbrella tore,* with the relative pronoun *that* replacing *The umbrella,* has become a _____

relative clause. ☐

Let's not worry too much about the terms *relative pronoun* and *relative clause.* Knowing how they work is enough.

The pen broke.

The pen wrote well.

Using *that,* embed the second sentence here into the first as a relative clause:

that wrote well broke *The pen* _____ . ☐

Other relative pronouns are the *who* family—*who, whose, whom.* And *that* is sometimes replaced by *which.*

The curtain rose slowly.

The curtain glittered.

Embed the second sentence into the first, using *which:*

which glittered *The curtain* _____ *rose slowly.* ☐

Let's return to our idea of focus. Remember, focus is always on the idea of the base sentence—the sentence into which others are embedded. In *The curtain which glittered rose slowly*, the base sentence is *The curtain (glittered, rose slowly)*. ☐

rose slowly

The movie played all week.

The movie has a biblical theme.

Using *that*, embed the first sentence into the second:

The movie _____

that played all week has

_____. ☐

a biblical theme

The movie that played all week has a biblical theme.

The focus here is on the (playing, theme). ☐

theme

In sentences about people, a form of *who (who, whose, whom)* acts as the relative pronoun instead of *which* or *that*.

The man came to the door.

The man sold brushes.

Using *who*, embed one sentence into the other to focus on the selling of brushes:

The man who _____

came to the door sold

_____. ☐

brushes

The child cried.

The child fell.

Embed one sentence into the other to focus on the crying:

_____ ☐

The child who fell cried.

Sometimes *whose* is necessary for embedding.

The players arrived late.

The players' bus broke down.

Embed the second sentence into the first:

The players whose _____ *arrived*

bus broke down

late. ☐

The girl's purse was stolen.

The girl called the police.

Embed one sentence into the other so that the focus is on calling the police. Use *whose.*

The girl whose purse was stolen called the police.

_____

_____ ☐

Occasionally *whom* is necessary for embedding:

A man became chairman.

I respect him.

To embed the second sentence into the first, we need *whom:*

whom I respect

A man _____ became chairman. ☐

The Smiths were there.

George knew the Smiths.

Using *whom*, embed to focus on the idea of place *(there):*

whom George knew, were there

The Smiths, _____ ,

_____. ☐

Notice that in some sentences we can embed with or without the relative pronoun.

The risk that he took was small.

The risk he took was small.

Even though the second sentence lacks the relative pronoun *that,*

is

it (is, is not) just as easily understood. ☐

The equipment which George carried was new.

which

In this sentence we can omit the relative pronoun _____. ☐

The people whom we met yesterday are all teachers.

Harry, whom I knew in high school, is now studying law.

In only one of these sentences can we leave out the relative

first

pronoun *whom*, the (first, second). ☐

The troop of Scouts helped with the fire fighting.

Mr. Simmons led the troop of Scouts.

Embed the second sentence into the first, this time not using the
relative pronoun:

The troop of Scouts _____

_____ . ☐

*Mr. Simmons led helped in the
fire fighting*

In those cases where the relative pronoun is optional, use it or not
as you wish. Remember that the important thing is focus.

Eighty-seven senators voted against the bill.

Eighty-seven senators had serious doubts.

Combine these sentences to focus on the vote:

Eighty-seven senators _____

_____

_____ . ☐

*Eighty-seven senators who had
serious doubts voted against
the bill.*

Now combine those same sentences to focus on the serious doubts:

_____

_____

_____ . ☐

*Eighty-seven senators who voted
against the bill had serious
doubts.*

The telephone repairmen went on strike.

The telephone repairmen demanded a 5 percent pay increase.

Focus on the striking:

_____

_____

_____ ☐

*The telephone repairmen who
demanded a 5 percent pay
increase went on strike.*

A while back we saw that sentences could be simply stitched
together by *and*. For instance, the last two sentences we worked
with could have been joined like this:

*The telephone repairmen went on strike, and they demanded
a 5 percent pay increase.*

But even though we now have just one sentence, the focus is
shared by two ideas, the strike and the demand for a

_____ . ☐

pay increase

Loggers had made the trail.

The hunters followed the trail.

Join these sentences with *and*. Use *it* in place of *the trail* the second time it appears.

Loggers had made the trail, and the hunters followed it.

_____

_____ □

Loggers had made the trail, and the hunters followed it.

The focus is divided between the making of the trail and the following of it. Using *that,* we can make a relative clause out of the second part:

the hunters followed

Loggers had made the trail that _____. □

Loggers had made the trail that the hunters followed.

The focus now is on only one idea, the making of the trail. Now rewrite the sentence so that the focus is on the following. Again, use *that.*

that loggers had made

The hunters followed the trail _____

_____. □

The bottle broke.

The bottle contained acid.

If we simply join these two sentences with *and,* we again have the problem of divided focus:

The bottle broke, and it contained acid.

Focusing on the breaking, we can rewrite the sentence this way:

contained acid

The bottle that _____ *broke.* □

The bottle contained acid.

The bottle broke.

Or we can focus on the contents:

that (which) broke contained acid

The bottle _____

_____. □

Whenever you find yourself using *and* to join sentences, see if it would be better to focus on one or the other of the ideas.

    My uncle came, and he is an engineer.

Rewrite this so that the focus is on the idea of being an engineer:

    My uncle _____ . ☐   *who came is an engineer*

    My uncle came, and he is an engineer.

Now rewrite it to focus on the coming:

    My uncle _____ . ☐   *who is an engineer came*

    The scaffolding supported the men, and it collapsed.

Rewrite this sentence to focus on the collapsing:

    The scaffolding _____   *that (which) supported the men*

_____ . ☐   *collapsed*

    The young salesman set two new sales records, and he was promoted to manager.

Rewrite to focus on the promotion:

    The young salesman _____   *who set two new sales records*

_____ . ☐   *was promoted to manager*

    The matches had gotten wet, and they refused to light.

Rewrite this to focus on the refusal to light:

    The matches _____   *that (which) had gotten wet*

_____ . ☐   *refused to light*

ADVERB CLAUSES

In this section we go on dealing with the question of focus because it is so important in the job of good sentence making. Now we'll look at the ways we can embed by using one other kind of clause, the adverb clause. And it's a lot simpler than it sounds because we're going to use the same principle we've been using; that is, to focus on an idea, we make that idea the base sentence.

We sang.

He played the piano.

Here are two sentences. Because they are separate, we don't think of the ideas of each as being necessarily related. Now let's join the two sentences with *and:*

and he played the piano

We sang, _____.□

We sang, and he played the piano.

Now the connection between the two ideas begins to appear. But we still think of the ideas as standing side by side, each receiving the focus of our attention in turn.

We sang while he played the piano.

But this sentence is different. Instead of *and,* the second sentence

while

is joined to the first by the word _____. □

While makes the sentence *He played the piano* part of the sentence *We sang.*

We sang while he played the piano.

While he played the piano, we sang.

does

Notice that the second arrangement here (does, does not) make as much sense as the first. □

We sang, and he played the piano.

And he played the piano, we sang.

does not

Now notice that the second arrangement here (does, does not) make as much sense as the first. □

And, then, can serve only to stitch two independent sentences together. *While,* on the other hand, makes one independent sentence a part of another.

> *I'll stay and you go.*
> *I'll stay if you go.*

In the second sentence *if* functions like *while* rather than like *and* because we (can, cannot) move *if you go* to come before *I'll stay.* ☐

can

While and *if* belong to a group of words called "subordinating conjunctions." Don't worry about the fancy name; just see how they work.

> *Harry left, and Charlie came.*

Using the subordinating conjunction *when,* make the second half of this sentence a part of the first:

> *Harry left* _____. ☐

when Charlie came

We can't say *And Charlie came, Harry left.* But we can reverse the parts of this sentence when it has the subordinating conjunction *when:*

> _____, *Harry left.* ☐

When Charlie came

There are many subordinating conjunctions in the language: *since, as, because, while, although,* and *where* are a few others.

> *The car skidded around the corner.*
> *It overturned.*

Make the first sentence here a part of the second, using *as:*

> *As* _____
>
> _____. ☐

the car skidded around the corner, it overturned

A sentence made part of another with a subordinating conjunction is called an "adverb clause."

> *As the car skidded around the corner, it overturned.*

In this sentence the adverb clause is the part (before, after) the comma. ☐

before

When Charlie came	In the sentence *When Charlie came, Harry left,* the adverb clause, introduced by the subordinating conjunction, is _____ _____. □
	Though an adverb clause usually comes before or after the base sentence to which it is attached, the process is still embedding because one independent sentence is made part of another. As a matter of fact, adverb clauses can often move around freely within a sentence.
	When they arrived, the Joneses honked the horn.
	The Joneses, when they arrived, honked the horn.
is	Even though we move the adverb clause *when they arrived* to the middle, the second sentence (is, is not) perfectly clear. □
	If it works, this radio has a good tone.
tone	We can move the adverb clause *If it works* to two other places in the sentence—after *radio* and after _____. □
	Make a slash mark in the two other places in the sentence where we can put the adverb clause *As you know:*
As you know, instant coffees / *are quite popular /.*	*As you know, instant coffees are quite popular.* □
	Let's return to the idea of focus. Remember the sentences we began with?
	We sang.
	He played the piano.
	Originally, we made the second sentence into an adverb clause introduced by *while:*
sang while he played the piano	We _____. □
	We sang while he played the piano.
	Here the base sentence is *We sang.* Now using *while* again, make the base sentence into an adverb clause joined to *He played the piano,* which will now become the base sentence:
played the piano while we sang	He _____ _____. □

We sang while he played the piano.

He played the piano while we sang.

Remember, the focus is always on the idea of the base sentence. In the first arrangement here, then, the focus is on the (singing, playing). In the second it is on the (singing, playing). □

singing   playing

While he played the piano, we sang.

Though the adverb clause now comes before the base sentence, the focus is on the (singing, playing). □

singing

With adverb clauses, however, we most often don't have a choice: focus is on one or the other of the sentences we need to combine.

You go.

I'll go.

Using *if* as our subordinating conjunction, there is only one way to combine these sentences:

If _____.□

you go, I'll go

If you go, I'll go.

Nevertheless, embedding has taken place. The base sentence is _____, and the adverb clause is _____. □

I'll go   If you go

The government canceled the contract, and he lost his job.

Here is a two-part sentence. Make one part into an adverb clause, using *after:*

_____

_____ □

After the government canceled the contract, he lost his job.

After the government canceled the contract, he lost his job.

Remember, the focus is on the idea of the base sentence. Here, then, the focus is on the idea of (contract cancellation, loss of job). □

loss of job

A twister roared through this Oklahoma city, and scores of people were injured.

Join the parts of this two-part sentence, focusing on the injuries. Use *when.*

When _____

_____

_____. ☐

a twister roared through this Oklahoma city, scores of people were injured

The party nominates Judge Aller, and it is certain to lose another election.

Rewrite to focus on the loss of the election. Use *if.*

_____

_____

_____ ☐

If the party nominates Judge Aller, it is certain to lose another election.

Let's go back to a rather important detail we skipped over a while back—the fact that adverb clauses are movable.

After she finished, she went home.

We can rewrite this sentence so that *After she finished* comes in another place:

_____

_____ ☐

She went home after she finished.

The normal place for an adverb clause is at the end of a sentence.

She went home after she finished.

is   Here the adverb (is, is not) in its normal place. ☐

The effect of moving an adverb clause from its normal place to come first in a sentence is to emphasize the entire sentence.

After she finished, she went home.

She went home after she finished.

first   The emphasized sentence is the (first, second). ☐

Emphasis is different from focus. Focus is always on the base sentence, no matter how the movable parts of a sentence are arranged. Emphasis depends on where we place movable parts.

The plate shattered as it fell.

As it fell, the plate shattered.

Both of these sentences have the same focus—the idea of shattering. But one is emphasized, the (first, second). ☐

second

To get a clear sense of how emphasis is different from focus, let's look at a very old joke, told in two different ways:

When he asked her, "Did you take a bus?" she said, "No, I didn't know one was missing."

She said, "No, I didn't know one was missing," when he asked her, "Did you take a bus?"

The funnier version is the (first, second). ☐

first

As the examples in the last frame show, the punch line of a joke has to come (first, last) in order for the joke to be funny. ☐

last

Humor depends on emphasis—that's why we put the punch line of a joke last. Similarly, when we combine sentences, we emphasize the new sentence by putting the embedded part first and the base sentence (the punch line) last.

The plane's landing lights had to be repaired before the flight could continue.

This sentence is unemphasized. In order to emphasize it, we would have to move a part to come first. Underline that part. ☐

before the flight could continue

After they had been in the sun all day, the crayons were melted into a useless blob of wax.

This sentence is (emphasized, unemphasized). ☐

emphasized

After they had been in the sun all day, the crayons were

melted into a useless blob of wax.

Rearrange the parts of this sentence so that it is not emphasized:

The crayons were melted into a

useless blob of wax after they

had been in the sun all day.

_____

_____

_____ ☐

Good writing contains relatively few emphasized sentences. When we write naturally and easily, the movable parts of sentences will tend most often to fall into normal positions. Only occasionally, for a special effect, will we emphasize a sentence.

The trumpet was stolen.

The musician left it in his unlocked car.

Combine these sentences to focus on the stealing. Place the adverb clause in its normal, unemphatic place:

The trumpet was stolen when

(because) the musician left it

in his unlocked car.

_____

_____

_____ ☐

NOUN CLUSTERS

Experienced writers have ways of combining sentences so that the focus is always where they want it. Not only do they use relative clauses and adverb clauses to combine sentences; they also use the four devices we're about to look at, the first of which is the noun cluster. Once again, don't let the unfamiliarity of the name bother you. As with the relative and adverb clauses, you'll find out you already know more than you realize about noun clusters as well as the other devices we're going to look at in the next sections.

A noun is a name word that usually has a plural form: *chair, chairs; robber, robbers.*

    The cat sat on the mat.

This sentence contains two nouns,_____ and _____. □   *cat mat*

In the following list, check all the nouns. Remember, only a noun can have a plural form ending in *s.*

    pencil   radio   so

    against   zebra   however □   *pencil radio zebra*

Nouns very seldom stand by themselves. For instance, the words *a, an,* and *the*—the so-called articles—always are related to nouns.

    The man had a child with him.

Here the article *The* is related to the noun _____, and the   *man*
article *a* is related to the noun _____. □   *child*

    The extremely old, gray-haired man had a child by the hand.
Between the article and its noun, any number of other words can appear, all related to the noun. Here the noun *man* has several words related to it: *the,* _____, _____, and   *extremely old*
_____. □   *gray-haired*

Words and groups of words related to a noun can also follow it.

The extremely old, gray-haired man with a bushy beard had a child by the hand.

In this sentence the words related to the noun *man* include all those up to the word _____.

had

A small wrench with a very short handle fits the lock bolt.

The words related to the noun *wrench* include all those up to the word _____. ☐

fits

Any group of words made up of a noun plus all the words related to it is called a noun cluster. *A small wrench with a very short handle,* then, is one example of a noun _____. ☐

cluster

The noun around which the related words are clustered is called the headword. The headword of *A small wrench with a very short handle* is not the noun *handle* but rather the noun _____. ☐

wrench

Underline the noun cluster in this sentence. Be sure to include all the words related to the noun.

The worn-out electrical transformer near the power plant is to be repaired. ☐

The worn-out electrical transformer near the power plant

The noun headword in *The worn-out electrical transformer near the power plant* is _____. ☐

transformer

A sentence can contain more than one noun cluster. Underline both noun clusters in this sentence:

The forty-two girls of the ballet company traveled in a single decrepit bus with worn tires. ☐

The forty-two girls of the ballet company
a single decrepit bus with worn tires

The noun headword of the first noun cluster in the last frame is _____. That of the second noun cluster is _____. ☐

girls   bus

Sometimes we have two noun clusters coming one after the other, both of them referring to the same person or thing.

>   *That man, a friend of mine, came in late.*

Here two noun clusters come one after the other. The headwords of both, *man* and *friend*, refer to (the same, different) person(s).☐   *the same*

When a second noun cluster in a sentence refers to the same person or thing, we call it an appositive. You probably remember the name from your school grammar.

>   *That man, a friend of mine, came in late.*

Here the appositive is *a friend of mine*. The headword of the appositive is _____. ☐   *friend*

>   *That man, a friend of mine, came in late.*

An appositive is in fact the result of embedding a noun cluster from another sentence. This sentence, for instance, comes from two sentences, *That man came in late* and *That man is a*

_____. ☐   *friend of mine*

A sentence following another can often be reduced to a noun cluster and embedded into the sentence it follows.

>   *The text was expensive. It was an economics book.*

The second sentence here has a noun cluster we can embed into the first:

>   *The text, _____, was expensive.* ☐   *an economics book*

>   *The text, an economics book, was expensive.*

The appositive in this sentence is *(The text, an economics book).* ☐   *an economics book*

>   *The newcomer relaxed in the lobby.*
>   *He was a loose-jointed young man of seventeen.*

We can combine these sentences by making the noun cluster in the second sentence an appositive in the first:

>   *The newcomer, _____,*
>   _____
>   _____.* ☐   *The newcomer, a loose-jointed young man of seventeen, relaxed in the lobby.*

Notice that noun clusters serving as appositives can move around in their sentence.

> A loose-jointed young man of seventeen, the newcomer relaxed in the lobby.

does This sentence (does, does not) make as much sense as the sentence in the last frame. □

> The rain, a blinding sheet of water, fell steadily.

Place the appositive at the end of the sentence:

The rain fell steadily, a blinding sheet of water.

_____

_____ □

> The soldier returned home.
> He was a prisoner of war for two years.

The second sentence here has a noun cluster we can use as an appositive in the first sentence, _____

a prisoner of war for two years

_____ . □

> The soldier returned home.
> He was a prisoner of war for two years.

We can take the noun cluster from the second sentence and embed it into the first sentence in any of three places: before _____,

The

soldier home after _____ , or after _____ . □

As we learned in the last section, we can emphasize an entire sentence by putting a movable part at the beginning of a sentence.

> A prisoner of war for two years, the soldier returned home.
> The soldier, a prisoner of war for two years, returned home.

first The emphasized arrangement here is the (first, second). □

Emphasis, remember, is different from focus. Emphasis depends on the arrangement of sentence parts.

> The dress, a vivid pink dinner gown, was striking.

Rearrange the parts so that the entire sentence is emphasized.

A vivid pink dinner gown, the _____ ,

dress was striking. _____ . □

Once again let's look at the idea of focus, remembering that focus is always on the idea of the base sentence.

The soldier, a prisoner of war for two years, returned home.

The base sentence is the one in which the appositive is embedded. The focus, then, is on (being a prisoner, returning home). ☐

returning home

The plane landed heavily. It was a Boeing 747.

Rewrite these two sentences as one, focusing on the landing:

_____

_____ ☐

The plane, a Boeing 747, landed heavily.

A sentence that can be reduced to a noun cluster and embedded into another sentence is often an afterthought, containing an idea that occurs to us after we have written the first sentence.

The yachts then turned for home. Frantically the crews unfurled the spinnakers. Spinnakers are large balloonlike sails.

Of the three sentences here, one is clearly an afterthought, the (second, third). ☐

third

Frantically the crews unfurled the spinnakers. Spinnakers are large balloonlike sails.

Here we can simply attach the noun cluster in the second sentence right to the first:

Frantically the crews unfurled the _____

_____. ☐

spinnakers, large balloonlike sails

The chairman called the meeting to order. Abruptly two men rose and asked to be heard. They were the mayor and the city manager.

Find the sentence containing the afterthought, reduce it to a noun cluster, and embed it in the preceding sentence as an appositive:

Abruptly two men, the mayor and the city manager, rose and asked to be heard.

_____

_____

_____ ☐

The rock musicians finished around two. They were a group of five young boys. Their manager called for them in a station wagon.

Find the sentence containing the afterthought and combine it with the preceding sentence:

The rock musicians, a group of five young boys, finished around two.

_____

_____

_____ ☐

ADJECTIVE CLUSTERS

Now we'll look at another detachable word group that we can embed into other sentences, the adjective cluster. Once again, the process of embedding allows us to place the focus where we want it.

Adjectives are descriptive words we use. Most often they are related to nouns, which they modify.

   The green dress is hers.

The descriptive word related to the noun *dress* in this sentence is

_____. ☐   *green*

Any descriptive word related to a noun is an adjective. *Green*, then, is an adjective.

   The long rowboat overturned.

In this sentence *long* is an _____ describing the noun   *adjective*

_____. ☐   *rowboat*

Adjectives have special characteristics: for instance, they have a form to indicate "more" and "most." *Green* has the forms *greener* (more) and *greenest* (most). *Long* has the forms *longer* (more) and _____ (most). ☐   *longest*

moreover	high	great
then	flag	late

Only three of the words in this list have forms to indicate "more" and "most": _____, _____, and _____. ☐   *high   great   late*

High, great, and *late,* then, are all (nouns, adjectives). ☐   *adjectives*

An adjective usually comes between an article *(a, an, the)* and the noun it is related to.

   The late train finally arrived.

Here the adjective *late* comes between the article *The* and the noun it is related to, _____. ☐   *train*

An adjective, however, does not have to appear between the article and the noun.

> *The train is late.*

Here the adjective *late* is separated from the noun it modifies, *train*, by the verb _____. □

is

As a matter of fact, adjectives can often appear apart from the nouns they modify. They can, for instance, come before the article.

> *Rotten, the stairs finally collapsed.*

Here the adjective *Rotten* modifies the noun it is separated from, _____. □

stairs

Other words sometimes cluster around adjectives, adding to their meaning:

> *Rotten from age and exposure, the stairs finally collapsed.*

Here the adjective *Rotten* has four words related to it:

_____, _____, _____, and _____. □

from age and exposure

As with the noun cluster we worked with in the last section, the adjective around which other words cluster is called the "head-word." In the adjective cluster *Rotten from age and exposure*, the adjective *Rotten* is the _____. □

headword

> *Weak from hilarious laughter, Chuck collapsed in the chair.*

Here the adjective cluster *Weak from hilarious laughter* has the adjective _____ as its headword. □

Weak

Notice also that adjective clusters move about more or less freely in a sentence:

> *Chuck, weak from hilarious laughter, collapsed in a chair.*
> *Chuck collapsed in a chair, weak from hilarious laughter.*

These versions of the sentence (do, do not) make as much sense as the version in the last frame. □

do

Rotten from age and exposure, the stairs finally collapsed.
We can place the adjective cluster *Rotten from age and exposure* in two other places in this sentence—after the word _____ and after the word _____. □

stairs

collapsed

The group, free after a year of hard work in VISTA, returned to their home cities.
This sentence has an unusually long adjective cluster, _____ _____.□

free after a year of hard work in VISTA

The group, free after a year of hard work in VISTA, returned to their home cities.
Though unusually long, the adjective cluster can be moved to two other positions—before the word _____ and after the word _____. □

The

cities

Adjective clusters, since they are movable, allow us to emphasize sentences in which they appear. Remember that we emphasize by putting a movable part at the beginning of the sentence.
Free after a year of hard work in VISTA, the group returned to their home cities.
This sentence, then, (is, is not) emphasized. □

is

The umbrella was torn and tattered.
The umbrella was the only object he carried.
We can embed the adjective cluster from the first sentence into the second:
The umbrella, _____ ,
was the only object he carried. □

torn and tattered

The umbrella, torn and tattered, was the only object he carried.
Because the movable part, the adjective cluster *torn and tattered*, does not come first, the sentence (is, is not) emphasized. □

is not

Rearrange the parts of the sentence in the last frame so that the sentence is emphasized:

Torn and tattered, the umbrella was the only object he carried.

_____ , _____

_____ . □

The child's eyes were wide open.
They were red from crying.

Here the second sentence is unnecessary because we can embed the adjective cluster from it into the first sentence:

red from crying, were wide open

The child's eyes, _____ ,

_____ . □

The child's eyes, red from crying, were wide open.

Rearrange the parts so that the sentence is emphasized:

Red from crying, the child's eyes were wide open.

_____

_____ □

For a moment, let's return to our idea of focus.

The child's eyes, red from crying, were wide open.

Since the focus in a sentence is always on the idea of the base sentence, here the focus is on the idea of the eyes' being (open,

open

red). □

Now let's go back to the original two sentences:

The child's eyes were wide open.
They were red from crying.

We can combine these sentences instead in a way that focuses on the idea of the eyes' being red:

were red from crying

The child's eyes, wide open, _____

_____ . □

The envelopes are large and brown.

They are unsuitable for our purposes.

Let's pick the adjective cluster out of the first sentence and embed it into the second:

The envelopes, large _____ , _____ *and brown, are unsuitable*

_____ .□ *for our purposes*

The envelopes, large and brown, are unsuitable for our purposes.

The focus here is on the envelopes' being (large and brown, unsuitable). □

unsuitable

The envelopes are large and brown. They are unsuitable for our purposes.

Now combine the sentences so that the focus is on their being large and brown:

The envelopes, _____ *unsuitable for our purposes,*

_____ , _____ .□ *are large and brown*

The four girls were ready to leave earlier.

They were angry at their dates.

Using the adjective cluster from one sentence, combine so that the focus is on the anger:

The four girls, _____ , *ready to leave earlier, were*

_____ .□ *angry at their dates*

The four girls were ready to leave earlier. They were angry at their dates.

Now combine to focus on the readiness to leave:

The four girls, _____ , *angry at their dates, were*

_____ .□ *ready to leave earlier*

As the example in the last frame shows, a sentence we can reduce to an adjective cluster is often an afterthought, something that occurred to the writer after he had finished the sentence into which he should have embedded it.

Professor Reid's philosophy attracted many students. It was boldly novel.

Combining these sentences allows us to put the afterthought into the sentence it belongs in:

boldly novel, attracted many students

Professor Reid's philosophy, _____ ,

_____ . ☐

The farmlands flooded often during the spring rains. They were rich with topsoil.

Combine these sentences, reducing the afterthought to an adjective cluster:

rich with topsoil, flooded often during the spring rains

The farmlands, _____ ,

_____ . ☐

The old coffeepot finally gave up. It was brown with rust.

Combine these sentences:

brown with rust, finally gave up

The old coffeepot, _____

_____ . ☐

The baby-sitter watched the girls dash around the bushes. They were full of mischief.

Combine these sentences:

the girls, full of mischief, dash around the bushes

The baby-sitter watched _____

_____ . ☐

VERB CLUSTERS

Another important group of devices we use to embed ideas into our sentences are the verb clusters. As you'll discover, though, you've probably seen these devices before, but under other names. Certainly you've used them, and probably without knowing it.

Let's begin here by being sure we know what a verb is. We could do that by going to one of the many definitions of the verb that have been concocted over the years. But since such definitions are almost totally useless, we won't bother. We don't need to because we have a simple way of instantly identifying a verb. It's this: all verbs, and only verbs, have a form to indicate past time. *Play* is a verb, and it has a form to indicate past time, *played*. *Open* is another verb; its past form is _____. ☐

opened

Not all past forms of verbs end in *-ed*. The past form of *see* is *saw*. The past form of *go* is _____. ☐

went

We have other ways to identify verbs, but we don't need them because this way is as sure as it is simple.

over	*give*	*run*
however	*weak*	*turn*

Only three of these words are verbs: _____, _____, and _____. ☐

give   run

turn

As you know from your school grammar, verbs play an important part in the formation of any sentence. That is, every complete sentence contains at least one verb.

   She left early.

The verb in this sentence is _____. ☐

left

   The plane turned and taxied to the hangar area.

This sentence has two verbs, _____ and _____. ☐

turned   taxied

Right now we're not interested in these verbs, the ones that make up the backbone of the sentence. Rather, we're interested in the forms that can be taken out of one sentence and embedded into another. One such is the form ending in *-ing*. *Giving* is the *-ing* form of *give*. The *-ing* form of *hurt* is _____. ☐

hurting

This *-ing* form has a fancy name—"present participle." But here, to keep it simple, we'll call it just the *-ing* form.

The water runs.

running

The verb in this sentence has an *-ing* form, _____. ☐

The water runs.

The water is hot.

We can easily embed the *-ing* form of the verb in the first sentence into the second:

running

The _____ water is hot. ☐

The leaves fall.

The leaves are red and brown.

We can embed the verb of the first sentence into the second by using its *-ing* form:

falling leaves are

The _____ red and brown. ☐

The embedded *-ing* form can often occupy other positions in the sentence:

The falling leaves are red and brown.

The leaves falling are red and brown.

does

Even though *falling* follows *leaves,* the second (does, does not) make the same kind of sense as the first. ☐

The *-ing* form of a verb can have other words related to it:

The leaves falling from the trees are red and brown.

from the trees

Here *falling* has three words related to it, _____

_____. ☐

Word groups based on the *-ing* form of verbs are called, you may remember, "participial phrases." Once again, though, let's keep it simple and just call it a "verb cluster." *Falling from the trees*, then, is an example of a _____. ☐

verb cluster

The verb is always the headword in a verb cluster. In *falling from the trees*, the headword is _____. ☐

falling

    He saw the children running from the bull.

In the verb cluster *running from the bull*, the *-ing* form *running* is the _____. ☐

headword

As we've already seen, having the *-ing* form of the verb available to us allows us to reduce a sentence to a word group we can embed into another sentence.

    The birds fly south.

    The birds avoid winter.

By changing *fly* to its *-ing* form, we can make the first sentence into a two-word verb cluster, _____. ☐

flying south

    The birds fly south.

    The birds avoid winter.

We can then fit the verb cluster from the first sentence into the second:

_____

_____

_____ ☐

Flying south, the birds avoid winter. Or: *The birds avoid winter flying south.*

    The team sensed victory.

    The team pressed even harder.

Change the verb of the first sentence into its *-ing* form and embed the verb cluster into the second sentence following *team:*

    The team, _____, _____

_____. ☐

sensing victory, pressed even harder

Charlie left home for good.

Charlie moved to Keene.

Once again, using the *-ing* device, embed the first sentence into the second. This time, let the verb cluster be the last part of the sentence.

to Keene, leaving home for good

Charlie moved _____

_____. ☐

A verb cluster is a movable part, so we can emphasize any sentence having one by putting it first.

Charlie moved to Keene, leaving home for good.

Rearrange the parts to emphasize the sentence:

Leaving home for good, Charlie moved to Keene.

_____

_____ ☐

The policeman approached the injured man.

He warned others away.

Embed the second sentence into the first so that the new sentence is emphasized:

Warning others away, the police-man approached the injured man.

_____

_____ ☐

The *-ing* form is only one of three verb forms we use as headwords in verb clusters. A second is the *-ed* form. The verb *defeat* has

cooked

the form *defeated;* the verb *cook* has the form _____. ☐

The army was defeated.

The army crossed the river.

The *-ed* form of the verb in the first sentence can be simply embedded in the second:

defeated army

The _____ *crossed the river.* ☐

Like the *-ing* form, the *-ed* form can move around in a sentence.

> *The defeated army crossed the river.*
>
> *Defeated, the army crossed the river.*
>
> *The army, defeated, crossed the river.*

Defeated can appear in yet another place in this sentence, after the word _____. ☐

         river

> *The cat was abandoned.*
>
> *The cat crept into the field.*

We can embed the *-ed* form of the verb in the first sentence into the second in several places. Here, embed it to follow *cat:*

> *The _____ , _____ , _____*
>
> *_____ .* ☐

         The cat, abandoned, crept into the field.

Just like the *-ing* form, the *-ed* form can serve as the headword in a verb cluster.

> *The cat was abandoned on the highway.*
>
> *The cat crept into the field.*

Embedding the first sentence into the second requires us to use all the words related to *abandoned:*

> *The cat, _____ ,*
>
> *crept into the field.* ☐

         abandoned on the highway

Abandoned on the highway, then, is a verb cluster. Its headword is _____. ☐

         Abandoned

> *The audience was startled out of its wits.*
>
> *The audience sat dumbfounded.*

Embed the verb cluster in the first sentence into the second sentence. Make it the first item:

> *_____ ,*
>
> *_____ .* ☐

         Startled out of its wits, the audience sat dumbfounded.

> *Startled out of its wits, the audience sat dumbfounded.*

We can move the verb cluster to one of two other places in the sentence, after *audience* and after _____. ☐

         dumbfounded

All verbs have a form ending in -*ing*. But not all verbs have a form ending in -*ed*. *Wait* has the form *waited*, but *throw* does not have a form *throwed*.

> *He has (throw) the ball.*

thrown | The form of *throw* to complete this sentence is _____. □

Though not all verbs have a form ending in -*ed*, all have a form we use with *have*. *Go, teach,* and *fight* are examples of verbs without a form ending in -*ed*, but they do have a form we use with *have:*

> *They have gone.*

taught | *They have (teach) _____.*

fought | *They have (fight) _____.* □

Since most verbs can take the -*ed* ending, we'll call the form of all verbs used with *have* the -*ed* form. Just remember that some do not end with the letters -*ed*, but have some special form of their own. With any verb, then, we can find the -*ed* form by putting it after *have*.

> *keep*   *catch*
>
> *wonder*   *amuse*

wonder | Only two of these verbs can take an -*ed* ending, _____

amuse | and _____. □

kept | *Keep* and *catch* have special -*ed* forms we can discover by using

them with *have: have (keep) _____* and *have (catch)*

caught | _____. □

Now let's get back to our main point: the -*ed* forms, like the -*ing* forms, can become headwords in a verb cluster we can embed into sentences.

> *Caught in the act, he pleaded guilty.*

Here we have a four-word verb cluster based on one of our irregu-

Caught in the act | lar -*ed* forms; the whole cluster is _____. □

The house, fallen into disrepair, could not be sold.

Here is another verb cluster based on an irregular *-ed* form. The

cluster is _____. ☐ | *fallen into disrepair*

Now let's do some more embedding.

> *The girls were stricken with flu.*

> *The girls missed a week of school.*

Embed the verb cluster in the first sentence into the second,

following *girls:*

> *The girls,* _____, | *The girls, stricken with flu,*

> _____. ☐ | *missed a week of school.*

> *The box served as a table.*

> *The box was emptied of its contents.*

Embed the verb cluster of the second sentence into the first. This

time, place it so that the new sentence is emphasized.

> _____, _____ | *Emptied of its contents, the box*

> _____. ☐ | *served as a table.*

> *The Volkswagen bus stood at the curb.*

> *It was covered with bright floral designs.*

Embed the second sentence into the first. This time, place the

verb cluster so that the sentence won't be emphasized.

> _____ | *The Volkswagen bus(,) covered*

> _____ | *with bright floral designs(,)*

> _____. ☐ | *stood at the curb.*

One other form of the verb can serve as the headword of a verb

cluster, the *to* form. *To buy, to run,* and *to write* are examples.

> *He wanted only to fish and to swim on his vacation.*

This sentence contains two *to* forms of verbs, _____ | *to fish*

and _____. ☐ | *to swim*

Bob practiced all week.

This was to win.

We can embed the *to* form in the second sentence into the first sentence:

To win   _____, Bob practiced all week. ☐

The children ran hard.

This was to keep up with the horse.

We can embed the verb cluster in the second sentence into the first:

To keep up with the horse   _____, the children ran hard. ☐

In order to embed one sentence into another using the *to* form, we often have to change the verb of the sentence we wish to embed into its *to* form.

We purified the water.

We added halazone tablets to it.

To purify the water   _____, we added halazone tablets to it. ☐

Bob proved his strength.

Bob lifted the heavy barrel.

To embed the first sentence into the second, we have to create a verb cluster by changing *proved* to its *to* form:

To prove his strength   _____, Bob lifted the heavy barrel. ☐

The fruit is shipped in refrigerated boxcars.

This keeps the fruit fresh.

Embed the second sentence into the first:

To keep the fruit fresh   _____, it is shipped in refrigerated boxcars. ☐

Like verb clusters with -*ing* and -*ed* forms as headwords, verb
clusters with *to* forms as headwords can also move around in a
sentence.

> *The directors avoided bankruptcy.*
> *The directors borrowed four million dollars.*

Using the *to* form, embed the first sentence into the second, this
time after *dollars:*

> *The directors borrowed* _____ | *four million dollars to*
>
> _____. ☐ | *avoid bankruptcy.*

> *The directors borrowed four million dollars to avoid*
> *bankruptcy.*

To emphasize this sentence, we would move *to avoid bankruptcy*
so that it comes before _____ . ☐   *The*

> *The hikers used their compass carefully.*
> *They found their way back to camp.*

Embed the second sentence into the first, using the *to* form.
Place the verb cluster after *hikers.*

> *The hikers,* _____ | *The hikers, to find their way*
>
> _____ | *back to camp, used their*
>
> _____. ☐ | *compass carefully.*

> *The hikers, to find their way back to camp, used their compass*
> *carefully.*

Now rearrange the parts to emphasize the sentence:

> _____ | *To find their way back to camp,*
>
> _____ | *the hikers used their compass*
>
> _____ ☐ | *carefully.*

ABSOLUTE PHRASES

One of the hallmarks of successful writing is the use of what are called "absolute phrases." Researchers have discovered that no other characteristic so clearly distinguishes the good writer from the beginner as the ability to use absolute phrases where needed. But since we normally do not use these devices in our everyday speech, beginners are often not aware of just how useful they are. Here, perhaps for the first time, you'll see how we form them and where we can use them to good advantage.

Remember the *-ing* form we dealt with in the last section? This form is the basis for one of the two most important kinds of absolute phrases we can use.

> *Rain threatened.*
> *We called the picnic off.*

The *-ing* form of the verb in the first sentence, *threatened*, is

threatening | _____. □

> *Rain threatened.*
> *We called the picnic off.*

We can't embed *threatening* in the second sentence by itself because we'd end up with nonsense: *Threatening, we called the picnic off.* We can, however, use it together with the other word related to it:

Rain | _____ *threatening, we called the picnic off.* □

Rain threatening is a structure called an "absolute phrase." Once again, don't worry about the fancy name. Just see what

threatening | it is. We have the *-ing* verb, _____, preceded by a noun, *Rain.* □

How do we know *rain* is a noun? Nouns, remember, have a form to indicate more than one. *Chair* is a noun because it has a form to indicate more than one, *chairs.* *Radio,* another noun, has the

rains | form *radios.* *Rain* has the form _____. □

The two kinds of absolute phrases we will be looking at all have at their core this combination, noun plus verb, here the *-ing* form.

Weather permitting, we'll reschedule the picnic for Saturday. This sentence contains an absolute phrase, _____ _____. ☐

Weather permitting

Though absolute phrases have a core of noun plus special verb form, they often have other words joined to them:

He left for home, his hopes rising rapidly. This sentence contains a four-word absolute phrase, *his hopes rising rapidly.* The core of it is the noun _____ and the *-ing* verb _____. ☐

hopes

rising

The man dashed for the bus, his coat flapping wildly in the wind.

This sentence contains a seven-word absolute phrase. But as always, the core is a noun, _____, and an *-ing* verb, _____. ☐

coat

flapping

Absolute phrases allow us to embed, not just part of a sentence, but an entire sentence into another.

The woman typed skillfully.

Her fingers flew over the keys.

We can make the second sentence into an absolute phrase by changing its verb, *flew,* to its *-ing* form, *flying.* Then we can embed it into the first sentence:

The woman typed skillfully, her fingers _____ _____. ☐

flying over the keys

The ambulance rushed down Sutter Street.

Its siren screamed loudly.

Change the verb in the second sentence, *screamed,* to its *-ing* form and embed the second sentence into the first sentence:

The ambulance rushed down Sutter Street, _____ _____. ☐

its siren screaming loudly

Usually absolute phrases can appear in any of several positions in a sentence.

The violinists played with great concentration.

Their bows moved in perfect unison.

We can make the second sentence into an absolute phrase by changing its verb to the *-ing* form. This time embed it into the first sentence to follow *violinists:*

their bows moving in perfect unison, played with great concentration

The violinists, _____

_____ , _____

_____ . □

The violinists, their bows moving in perfect unison, played with great concentration.

We can move the absolute phrase in this sentence to two other positions, to come before *The* and to come after

concentration

_____ . □

The violinists, their bows moving in perfect unison, played with great concentration.

Rearrange the parts to emphasize the sentence:

Their bows moving in perfect unison, the violinists played with great concentration.

_____

_____

_____ □

The speaker tried to quiet the crowd.

His voice rose to a shout.

Make the second sentence into an absolute phrase and embed it into the second sentence. This time make it the last element in the sentence.

The speaker tried to quiet the crowd, his voice rising to a shout.

_____ ,

_____

_____ . □

Sometimes a sentence we want to make into an absolute phrase will already have the *-ing* verb. In such cases, it will always follow a form of *be (are, is, was, were)*. All we have to do is remove the *be* word and we have a ready-made absolute phrase.

> *The cyclist pulled off the road.*
> *His engine was sputtering.*

To make the second sentence into an absolute phrase, we simply cross out the *be* word, which here is _____. □   *was*

> *The cyclist pulled off the road.*
> *His engine was sputtering.*

Embed the second sentence into the first, placing it to emphasize the new sentence:

_____   *His engine sputtering, the*

_____ □   *cyclist pulled off the road.*

The one other form of the verb that can serve as the basis for absolute phrases is the *-ed* form.

> *She worked hard at the task.*
> *Her brow was furrowed.*

Notice that the second sentence already has the *-ed* form of the verb. Just cross out *was,* and the second sentence becomes an absolute phrase we can embed into the first:

> *She worked hard at the task, her* _____. □   *brow furrowed*

Sentences we can make into absolute phrases with *-ed* verbs always will have that form following a form of *be (are, is, was, were).* To make the absolute phrase, we remove the *be* word.

> *They sat talking in a corner.*
> *Their voices were muted.*

Here we cross out *were* to make the second sentence an absolute phrase we can embed in the first:

> *They sat talking in a corner,* _____   *their voices muted*

_____. □

His work was finished.

He left for the day.

Make the first sentence into an absolute phrase and embed it into the second. This time, place the absolute phrase to emphasize the sentence.

His work finished, he left for the day.

_____,

_____. ☐

Be alert to which verb form to use, the *-ing* or *-ed* form. Only if the verb follows a form of *be (is, are, was, were)* can we use the *-ed* form. In all other cases, we use the *-ing* form.

The tree seemed alive.

Its branches waved in the high wind.

Since the verb of the second sentence does not follow a *be* word, we have to change it to its *-ing* form before we can embed it into the first sentence:

Its branches waving in the high wind

_____,

the tree seemed alive. ☐

The skiers flew down the slope.

Their paths were marked clearly in the new snow.

Here, since the verb in the second sentence follows a *be* word, we can make an absolute phrase without changing the verb form:

The skiers flew down the slope, their paths marked clearly in the new snow.

The skiers _____,

_____

_____. ☐

The television was repaired.

We were able to watch the game.

Make the first sentence into an absolute phrase and embed it into the second:

The television repaired, we were able to watch the game.

The television _____ , _____

_____.☐

The garden was a mess.

Tall weeds grew everywhere.

Make the second sentence into an absolute phrase and embed it into the first, placing it so that the new sentence is emphasized:

_____ ,

_____ □

Tall weeds growing everywhere, the garden was a mess.

Let's do one more.

The Japanese tourists came down the ramp.

Their faces were shining.

Embed the second sentence into the first wherever you want:

_____

_____ □

Their faces shining, the Japanese tourists came down the ramp. Or: *The Japanese tourists, their faces shining, came down the ramp.* Or: *The Japanese tourists came down the ramp, their faces shining.*

REVIEW: SENTENCES

Before going on, let's put together what we've learned in Part Two, Sentences. We've looked at and learned to use the basic tools for embedding a part or all of one sentence into another. The purpose of embedding is, as we saw, partly to avoid using unnecessary words. But mostly, embedding allows us to focus on the particular idea or ideas we want to keep uppermost n our readers' minds. Writing strings of sentences without focus is like giving a guided tour without identifying major points of interest. The good writer, like the good tour guide, helps us find our way surely along the unfamiliar terrain of his ideas.

Focus is what sentence writing is all about. When a writer puts a period at the end of a sentence, he says in effect that the idea of that sentence has equal weight with the idea of any other sentence.

> *John came. Jack went.*

have | Here John's coming and Jack's going (have, have not) equal weight. ☐

Joining sentences with *and* has the same effect, though less obviously.

> *John came, and Jack went.*

The ideas of the two sentences now joined by *and* still have

equal | (equal, unequal) weight or focus. ☐

You've heard people whose conversations are just a string of sentences joined by *and*.

> *Helen is visiting us, and she is my cousin, and she lives in*
> *Albany, and she goes to Syracuse, and she is majoring in*
> *journalism.*

If you're trying to figure out what the person is trying to say, you're in for trouble. The problem is that the speaker unwitting-

and | ly gives equal focus to each of the ideas joined by _____. ☐

> *Helen, my cousin who lives in Albany, is visiting us. She goes to Syracuse, where she is majoring in journalism.*

This is probably what Gushy Gertie, who produced the sentence in the last frame, was trying to say. She used *and* four times. How many times does it appear here? _____ □

Not once.

Now of course there's nothing wrong with *and*. When we have two or more closely related ideas that we want to share equal focus, it's the ideal link.

> *Her purse was green. Her shoes were red.*
>
> *Her purse was green. She sat on the bench.*

Only one of these pairs of sentences has ideas closely enough related to be joined by *and*, the (first, second) pair. □

first

> *The car stopped. Two men climbed out.*
>
> *The car stopped. Four children were playing nearby.*

We would join only one of these sentence pairs with *and*, the (first, second) pair. □

first

The principle we are seeing in operation here is simple. When we want the idea of one sentence to be in focus by itself, we do not join it to another sentence.

> *The car stopped. Two men got out.*

If we want the ideas in each of these sentences to be separately in focus, we (will, will not) join them with *and*. □

will not

Sentences having closely related ideas that we want to share equal focus will be joined by *and*.

> *The car stopped. Two men got out.*

Revise these sentences so that they share equal focus.

_____ □

The car stopped, and two men got out.

Let's go back to the very first way of embedding we looked at in this section.

> *The building is tall. It is new.*
>
> *The building is tall, and it is new.*

Neither of these arrangements is satisfactory. Unless the writer has some peculiar reason why each sentence must be in focus by itself or share equal focus, he will embed the idea of one sentence into the other. He will, for instance, embed the idea of the second into the first:

new | *The _____ building is tall.* □

> *The building is tall. It is new.*

The other way is to embed the first sentence into the second:

building is new | *The tall _____ .* □

Keep in mind what we've seen earlier: focus is always on the idea of the base sentence, which is the sentence into which we embed parts or all of other sentences. In *The tall building is new,* the

The building is new. | base sentence is *(The building is tall, The building is new).* □

> *She tried on two dresses, and they were green.*

Here two sentences are spliced together with *and.* Make the first the base sentence and embed the idea following *and* into it:

two green dresses | *She tried on _____ .* □

> *The visitors are there, and they are ready for the meeting.*

Again we have a sentence made of two sentences joined by *and.* Make the second element the base:

there are ready for the meeting | *The visitors _____ .* □

Another device we've looked at that allows us to focus on one idea is the relative clause. Using *who (whose, whom), which,* or *that,* we can often make a separate sentence part of another.

> *Some members wanted a postponement.*
>
> *They had serious questions.*

Using *who,* we can embed the second sentence into the first:

had serious questions wanted a | *Some members who _____*

postponement | *_____ .* □

*Some members who had serious questions wanted a postpone-
ment.*

The focus in this version is on the (questions, postponement). ☐   *postponement*

Some members wanted a postponement.

They had serious questions.

Now write a version focusing on the questions:

The members _____   *who wanted a postponement had*

_____. ☐   *serious questions*

Using the relative clause device can permit us to escape the
clumsy *and* splicing of sentences.

The manufacturers had confidence in the motor, and they were
ready to market it.

Using *who,* rewrite this sentence to focus on the readiness to market the motor:

The manufacturers, _____   *who had confidence in the motor,*

_____, _____. ☐   *were ready to market it*

The manufacturers had confidence in the motor, and they
were ready to market it.

Now write a version focusing on the confidence, again using *who.*

The manufacturers _____   *who were ready to market the*

_____. ☐   *motor had confidence in it*

The studio produced one movie, and it was rated GP.

Using *which* or *that,* write a version focusing on the production
of one movie:

The studio _____   *produced one movie that*

_____. ☐   *(which) was rated GP*

The registrar hired four girls, and they needed part-time work.

Write a version focusing on the hiring:

The registrar _____   *hired four girls who needed*

_____. ☐   *part-time work*

In his speech today Senator Burns singled out high wages as the major cause of inflation, and he has spoken on economic problems regularly.

This is a somewhat longer sentence, but the principle of embedding still applies. Write a version focusing on the singling out of high wages:

who has spoken on economic problems regularly, singled out high wages as the major cause of inflation

In his speech today Senator Burns, _____

_____, _____

_____. □

Another way we can focus our sentences is by using adverb clauses. As we have seen, adverb clauses are sentences we embed into others using words we call subordinating conjunctions *(since, until, if, because,* and others).

Bob stayed home. He wasn't ready.

We can embed the second sentence into the first, using *because:*

because he wasn't ready

Bob stayed home _____

_____. □

Bob stayed home because he wasn't ready.

Bob stayed home.

The base sentence here is *(Bob stayed home, He wasn't ready).* □

The patrol car sped away. Its driver was ordered to an accident.

Join these sentences to focus on the speeding away. Use *when.*

sped away when its driver was ordered to an accident

The patrol car _____

_____. □

Adverb clauses permit us to avoid awkward *and* splices.

You fail to add oil, and you'll ruin the engine.

Write a version focusing on ruining the engine:

If you fail to add oil, you'll ruin the engine. Or: *You'll ruin the engine if you fail to add oil.*

_____,

_____

_____. □

She finished, and she called us immediately.

Write a version focusing on the calling. This time, place the adverb clause first to emphasize the new sentence.

_____,

_____. □

When she finished, she called us immediately.

Now let's look again at noun clusters. Remember, they're groups of words clustered around a noun that we can pluck out of one sentence and put into another.

We drove to the orchard.

It was a large grove of pear trees.

The second sentence has a noun cluster based on *grove*. We can embed it into the first sentence:

We drove to the orchard, _____

_____. □

a large grove of pear trees

We drove to the orchard, a large grove of pear trees.

The base sentence here is *(We drove to the orchard, It was a large grove of pear trees).* □

We drove to the orchard.

The range officer was worried about the test.

He was the senior official on the project.

Use the first sentence as the base sentence and embed the noun cluster in the second sentence into it:

The range officer, _____

_____, _____. □

the senior official on the project, was worried about the test

Marijuana is not technically a narcotic.

It is a drug.

Join these sentences to focus on the idea of marijuana not being a narcotic:

Marijuana, _____, _____

_____. □

a drug, is not technically a narcotic

Marijuana, a drug, is not technically a narcotic.

Now rearrange the parts of this sentence to emphasize it:

A drug, marijuana is not technically a narcotic.

_____

_____ ☐

Adjective clusters, like noun clusters, are groups of words related to adjectives. As with a noun cluster, we can embed an adjective cluster from one sentence into another sentence to place the focus where we need it.

The rancher worried about the cold weather.

He was tired from overwork.

We can embed the adjective *tired* and its related words into the first sentence:

tired from overwork

The rancher, _____,

was worried about the cold weather. ☐

The rancher, tired from overwork, was worried about the cold weather.

worried   The focus here is on the rancher's being (tired, worried). ☐

Charlie was handsome in a rugged sort of way, and he wanted to be an actor.

Write a version focusing on Charlie's wanting to be an actor:

handsome in a rugged sort of

way, wanted to be an actor

Charlie, _____

_____ . ☐

The merchandise was carefully labeled, and it was ready for delivery.

Write a version focusing on its being carefully labeled:

ready for delivery, was carefully

labeled

The merchandise, _____,

_____ . ☐

The merchandise, ready for delivery, was carefully labeled.

Now rearrange the parts to emphasize the sentence:

Ready for delivery, the merchan-

dise was carefully labeled.

_____

_____ ☐

Like noun and adjective clusters, verb clusters allow us to avoid clumsy, unfocused sentences and sentence sequences. There are three kinds of verb clusters, remember: one based on *-ing* verbs, one on *-ed* verbs, and one on *to* verbs.

The four men, trying to lift the piano, finally gave up.
Here, the verb cluster is based on the (*-ing*, *-ed*, *to*) verb form. ☐   *-ing*

The four men, trying to lift the piano, finally gave up.
The focus here is on the (trying, giving up). ☐   *giving up*

Each of the children wanted a chance to play, and they were standing in line.
Focus on the children's wanting a chance to play. Embed the *-ing* verb cluster.

Each of the children _____   *standing in line wanted a*

_____ . ☐   *chance to play*

The water was polluted badly, and it was unfit for drinking.
Using the *-ed* verb cluster, embed to focus on the water's being unfit for drinking:

The water, _____   *polluted badly, was unfit for*

_____ . ☐   *drinking.*

The water, polluted badly, was unfit for drinking.
Rearrange the parts for emphasis:

_____   *Polluted badly, the water was*

_____ ☐   *unfit for drinking.*

The verb cluster based on the *to* form of the verb can be handled in the same way as the other kinds.

You turn left here, and you can find the market.
Use the *to* form to make a verb cluster of the second part:

You turn left here _____ . ☐   *to find the market*

I called the reporter, and I straightened the story out.

Write a version focusing on the calling. Use the *to* form of the verb.

the reporter to straighten the

story out

I called _____

_____ . ☐

I called the reporter to straighten the story out.

Rearrange the parts for emphasis:

To straighten the story out, I

called the reporter.

_____

_____ ☐

Absolute phrases, as we saw, are like verb clusters except that they have a noun coming before the *-ing* or *-ed* verb.

As usual, O'Hare field was crowded, and planes were taxiing everywhere.

We can focus on the field's being crowded by changing the part after *and* to an absolute phrase based on the noun *planes* and the *-ing* verb:

taxiing everywhere

As usual, O'Hare field was crowded, planes _____

_____ . ☐

The hard-hats worked steadily, and their rivet guns clattered.

Focus on the working by making the part following *and* into an absolute phrase. Remember to change the verb to its *-ing* form.

their rivet guns clattering

The hard-hats worked steadily, _____

_____ . ☐

Death Valley is a wasteland, and its sand is bleached white.

Here we can focus on the idea of a wasteland by making the part after *and* into an absolute phrase based on the *-ed* verb.

is a wasteland, its sand bleached

white

Death Valley _____

_____ . ☐

Death Valley is a wasteland, its sand bleached white.

Rearrange the parts for emphasis:

_____

_____ ☐

Its sand bleached white, Death Valley is a wasteland.

THREE
PARAGRAPHS

Paragraphs are basic to writing. Seldom, if ever, do we write sentences by themselves. Instead, we write sequences of many sentences, each one connected to other sentences in a way that spreads out in front of our reader all the individual ideas that add up to the point we are making. Putting sentences together in paragraphs, then, is probably the most important part of writing.

GENERAL AND PARTICULAR STATEMENTS

The first and most important step in learning how to write paragraphs is learning the difference between general and particular statements. A general statement is one that can summarize several particular statements.

Our air contains harmful chemicals.

Our water is often impure.

Our environment is polluted.

One of these statements is a summary statement covering the other two, the (first, second, third). □

third

Our environment is polluted is a general statement because it summarizes the two particular statements. Let's look at another group.

> *Prices are rising.*
> *The cost of food is rising.*
> *Building costs are rising.*

The general statement here, summarizing the other two, is the

first   (first, second, third). ☐

Particular statements are those summarized by a general statement.

> *Women's fashions have changed rapidly.*
> *Pantsuits have become popular.*
> *Lipstick is again widely used.*

Since they are summarized by the first statement, the second and

particular   third statements here are (particular, general) statements. ☐

> *Fair employment practices are not yet a reality in this country.*
> *Racial minorities do not have equal opportunities in hiring and promotion.*
> *Women often receive lower wages than men doing similar work.*

first   The general statement here is the (first, second, third). The two

second and third   particular statements are (the first and second, the second and third). ☐

Keep in mind the simple principle that a general statement summarizes particular statements.

> *War kills and injures indiscriminately.*
> *It is extremely costly.*
> *Recovery is painful and often prolonged.*
> *In these ways war is like an illness.*

general   The last statement here is (general, particular). The first three

particular   are (general, particular). ☐

We can know if a statement is general or particular only by comparing it with other statements related to it. A statement is more general if it covers more than a related statement.

All dogs have fleas.

My dog Herman has more than his share.

Since *All dogs* refers to many more dogs than *My dog Herman*, the first statement here is more (general, particular) than the second. □ | *general*

"Sesame Street" teaches children basic skills.

Television shows are sometimes educational.

Since the first statement here covers less—one television show—than the second statement, it is (more, less) particular than the second. □ | *more*

Finding something valuable is always a pleasant surprise.

Yesterday I found a ten-dollar bill in an old purse.

Since *something valuable* can refer to more than *ten-dollar bill*, the more general statement here is the (first, second). □ | *first*

Drug addiction is often fatal.

Hard drug users run the most serious risks.

Here the first statement is more general than the second because *Drug* can refer to (more, fewer) kinds of drugs than *Hard drugs*. □ | *more*

Drug addiction is often fatal.

Hard drug users run the most serious risks.

Heroin addicts almost always have very short lives.

Since there are other kinds of hard drugs besides heroin, *Hard drug users* covers more than *Heroin addicts*. Therefore, the third statement is more (particular, general) than the second. □ | *particular*

In the last frame we saw three statements, the second more particular than the first and the third more particular than the second.

> *The Volkswagen is extremely popular.*
> *Foreign cars sell well in the United States.*
> *Imported products of all kinds have a large share of the American market.*

particular

In this sequence the first statement is more particular than the second, and the second is more (particular, general) than the third. ☐

By now you should be able to tell which statements in a sequence are more particular or more general than others. To keep you honest, we'll now go over a scrambled sequence:

> *Some materials shrink more than others.*
> *Even some kinds of cotton shrink more than other kinds.*
> *Cotton shrinks more than rayon.*

first

second

The most general is the (first, second, third). The most particular is the (first, second, third). ☐

Let's look at another scrambled sequence:

> *Foods containing the minerals potassium and magnesium should be a regular part of the diet.*
> *A person's diet should contain all essential minerals.*
> *Magnesium particularly is an important daily need.*

This time number the sentences: most general, 1; less general, 2;

2, 1, 3

least general, 3. ☐

Here is a scrambled four-sentence sequence. Number the sentences from most general (1) to least general (4).

> *Football is the most popular of the televised sports.*
> *Televised sports programs have large audiences.*
> *The largest single audience for a televised sports show is the one that watches professional football's annual Super Bowl.*
> *More people watch professional football games than any*

2, 1, 4, 3

other televised sports event. ☐

Let's go over another sequence in the same way:

Heat and noise are two of the worst reducers of efficiency.

The surroundings a person works in will affect his efficiency.

Noise particularly, since it speeds fatigue, is probably the worst offender.

Unpleasant surroundings can reduce a person's efficiency, sometimes drastically. □   *3, 1, 4, 2*

The following frames have similar sequences. Go over them carefully just to be sure you understand completely what we've been doing so far in this section. Number the statements as before.

We fear all kinds of things, from unfriendly dogs to death itself.

Our fear arises from the things that threaten—or seem to threaten—us.

Fear is an all-pervasive human emotion.

Fear of death seems to trouble all of us except the very young. □   *3, 2, 1, 4*

The inner city of New York has problems so deep that only massive effort can solve them.

The inner cities of America are in deep trouble.

The larger an inner city is, the more its trouble is.

The large inner cities of Boston and New York are in the worst shape. □   *4, 1, 2, 3*

Because of long-standing prejudices, a person's job defines his social status.

Doctors claim the highest pay and the highest status in our society.

The highest pay and the highest status usually go to professional work—medicine and law.

Generally, though not always, the higher the pay, the more status a job has. □   *1, 4, 3, 2*

TOPIC SENTENCES

Almost all the paragraphs we write contain one statement more general than the other statements in the paragraph. We have a name for that general statement—the "topic sentence." Usually the topic sentence is the first sentence in the paragraph, though not always. But it will always be the most general statement in the paragraph.

To begin, let's return to a subject we dealt with when we were talking about words: the difference between abstract and concrete words. We saw then that words are abstract if they refer to relatively more persons or things than other words. To take an example we've already used, the word *machine* is more abstract

more | than *typewriter* because it refers to (more, fewer) things. ☐

Choose the more abstract word in the following pairs:

car	*milk*	*clothes*

car drink clothes | *Ford* | *drink* | *sweater* ☐

Words are concrete if they refer to relatively fewer persons or things than other words. Compared with *car, drink,* and *clothes,*

concrete | the words *Ford, milk,* and *sweater* are (concrete, abstract). ☐

abstract | *Tree* is more (concrete, abstract) than *pine; baby* is more
concrete | (abstract, concrete) than *person.* ☐

So far we have been dealing only with single words more concrete or abstract than others. There is a way, however, to make the same word more concrete, and that is to add other words to it. *Dress,* for instance, is fairly abstract because there are all kinds of dresses to which it could refer; *green dress* is more concrete than *dress* because it refers to (more, fewer) things

fewer | than *dress* by itself. ☐

We can, of course, add more than one word to another. The more we add, the more concrete it becomes.

a blue car

a light blue car

a light blue car with racing slicks

The second phrase is more concrete than the (first, third), and the third is more concrete than (the first, both first and second). ☐

first

both first and second

Take the word *door* and make it as concrete as you can by adding words to it:

_____

_____

_____ ☐

The heavy green metal cabinet

door with brass hinges and

glass knobs is a sample.

Keeping the distinction between concrete and abstract words in the front of our minds, let's go back to the distinction we've just looked at, between general and particular statements.

Prices are rising.

The cost of food is rising.

Building costs are rising.

Remember that we identified the first of these statements as more (general, particular) than the other two. ☐

general

When a statement is more general than others related to it, it will have at least one key word more abstract than similar key words in the related statements.

Prices are rising.

The cost of food is rising.

Building costs are rising.

Because it can refer to more things, *Prices,* the key word in the first statement, is more (concrete, abstract) than either *cost of food* or *Building costs.* ☐

abstract

Here's another group we looked at:

Our environment is polluted.

Our air contains harmful chemicals.

Our water is impure.

We saw that the most general statement among these is the (first, second, third). ☐

first

Our environment is polluted.

Our air contains harmful chemicals.

Our water is impure.

The key word in the first and most general statement is *environment*. Because it can also refer to such things as *city streets* and *countryside* besides *air* and *water*, *environment* is more (abstract, concrete). ☐

abstract

Most topic sentences have one word or phrase more abstract than others. This word or phrase is the key to the rest of the paragraph.

George wears odd clothes.

The most abstract word or phrase in this sentence is not *George* but the two-word phrase _____. ☐

odd clothes

We'll call the most abstract word or phrase in the topic sentence the key.

George wears odd clothes.

If this is the topic sentence of a paragraph, *odd clothes* is the

_____. ☐

key

A paragraph, of course, has more than just a key. It has a topic also—who or what the paragraph is about.

George wears odd clothes.

The paragraph a sentence like this begins will be about George. George, then, will be the _____ of the paragraph. ☐

topic

Topic plus key—that's the simple formula for a successful topic sentence.

Rats are disease carriers.

If this were the topic sentence, we would expect the paragraph to be about not chickens or goats, but _____. ☐ | *rats*

Rats are disease carriers.

Each of the sentences of the paragraph this topic sentence introduces would be about rats. Rats, then, would be the _____ | *topic*
of the paragraph. ☐

Rats are disease carriers.

What about rats? That's the question the key of the topic sentence answers. Rats carry disease. The key in this topic sentence, then, is the two-word phrase _____. ☐ | *disease carriers*

Though fairly concrete, *disease carriers* can refer to more than the phrase *carriers of bubonic plague* or *carriers of typhoid fever*, two serious health dangers of rats. Compared with these last two phrases, *disease carriers* is more (concrete, abstract). ☐ | *abstract*

When we write a topic sentence, we have no difficulty usually in deciding on the topic of the paragraph. But if we try to write a topic sentence without first knowing what we are going to say about the topic, we cannot write a successful key.

Rats are a menace.

Suppose this was the topic sentence. The key now is

_____. ☐ | *a menace*

Rats are a menace for many more reasons than their being disease carriers. They destroy food; they attack and have actually killed children. If the paragraph we want to write has to do only with their being disease carriers, *a menace* is too (abstract, concrete) to be a good key. ☐ | *abstract*

On the other hand, we can have a key that is too concrete.

Rats are carriers of bubonic plague.

This would be a poor topic sentence for a paragraph on rats as disease carriers because rats carry other diseases besides bubonic plague. The key in this sentence, *bubonic plague,* is *concrete* too (abstract, concrete). ☐

The idea is simple: the key of a topic sentence should be just abstract enough to include the specific things the paragraph says about the topic.

What children eat for breakfast is important.
What children eat for breakfast can determine how well they function in school.
What children eat for breakfast can determine how easily they can learn the sets theory.

Here are three possible topic sentences. If the paragraph is to be about the connection between nutrition and a child's ability to perform his schoolwork, the first sentence would be a poor topic sentence because its key, *important,* is too (abstract, *abstract* concrete). ☐

What children eat for breakfast can determine how well they function in school.
What children eat for breakfast can determine how easily they can learn the sets theory.

Schoolwork includes much more than learning the sets theory. The last sentence here would not be a good topic sentence for the paragraph because its key, *how easily they can learn the concrete sets theory,* is too (abstract, concrete). ☐

What children eat for breakfast can determine how well they function in school.

This would be a good topic sentence because its key, _____

_____ ,

is just abstract enough to cover the ideas of the paragraph. ☐

how well they function in school

Hard-hats, the skilled construction workers of America, have interesting political views.

Hard-hats, the skilled construction workers of America, have a relatively conservative political outlook.

Of the keys in these two sentences, *interesting political views* and *a relatively conservative political outlook,* the more abstract is the (first, second). ☐

first

Hard-hats, the skilled construction workers of America, have a relatively conservative political outlook.

Hard-hats, the skilled construction workers of America, have strong feelings about honoring the flag.

Of the keys in these two sentences, *a relatively conservative political outlook* and *strong feelings about honoring the flag,* the second is more (concrete, abstract). ☐

concrete

Hard-hats, the skilled construction workers of America, have interesting political views.

Hard-hats, the skilled construction workers of America, have a relatively conservative political outlook.

Hard-hats, the skilled construction workers of America, have strong feelings about honoring the flag.

In a paragraph about the way hard-hats view the Democratic and Republican parties, the best topic sentence would be the (first, second, third). ☐

second

Once we have chosen the topic of a paragraph, we need to be sure the topic sentence contains a key that will just cover what the paragraph will say about the topic.

> *Our city parks contain (too little play equipment, too few swings, too little for amusement).*

For a paragraph on the lack of various kinds of things children use for play in parks, the best key would be the (first, second, third). ☐

first

> *When naming a child, almost all parents in our society prefer (names like Tom and Barbara, traditionally accepted names, names of a particular kind).*

For a paragraph that shows how parents tend to choose familiar names rather than unfamiliar or invented names for their children, the best key would be the (first, second, third). ☐

second

> *The frightening fact is that firearms of all kinds are (often purchased, relatively inexpensive, available to almost anyone).*

For a paragraph showing that there are no effective controls over who buys guns, the best key would be the (first, second, third). ☐

third

> *Although local, state, and federal governments are trying to improve the situation, our cities are rapidly becoming (very dirty, unsuitable places to live and work, places where all kinds of changes are occurring).*

For a paragraph describing how ordinary life is becoming more difficult in large cities, the best key would be the (first, second, third). ☐

second

PARAGRAPH DEVELOPMENT

Now that you know what makes a good topic sentence, we can look at the ways we put sentences together with them to make paragraphs. As you will see, all the sentences in a paragraph are related in a way that guides your reader step by step through the details of your ideas about a particular topic. The topic sentence, with its topic and key, acts as a base to hold the paragraph together.

Let's start with the first and simplest topic sentence we looked at in the last section:

George wears odd clothes.

In this topic sentence, *George* is the _____, and *odd clothes* is the _____. □

topic
key

We'll add one sentence to this topic sentence:

George wears odd clothes. **In most weather he dresses in a pair of striped coveralls cut off at the knees.**

Notice the relationship between *odd clothes,* the key, and the phrase *a pair of striped coveralls cut off at the knees.* Since the phrase in the new sentence refers to a particular kind of odd clothing, it is more (concrete, abstract). □

concrete

What we do in a paragraph is give concrete details of the key in the topic sentence.

George wears odd clothes. In most weather he dresses in a pair of striped coveralls cut off at the knees. **Sometimes he adds a red beret.**

Here we've added another sentence, with a detail as concrete as *a pair of striped coveralls cut off at the knees:* _____. □

red beret

George wears odd clothes. In most weather he dresses in a pair of striped coveralls cut off at the knees. Sometimes he adds a red beret. **When it rains, he drapes himself with an old army poncho.**

Here we've added a sentence with still another concrete detail of the (topic, key) *odd clothes: an old army poncho.* □

key

We could go on adding sentences to this paragraph, each one having more concrete details about George's odd clothes. But for a moment let's look at the ways a paragraph can go wrong.

George drives a red and yellow striped Volkswagen.

We would not add this sentence to the paragraph. Though it is about George, the concrete detail, *a red and yellow striped*

is not | Volkswagen, (is, is not) related to the key *odd clothes.* ☐

Charlie, George's friend, also wears odd clothes.

This sentence follows *odd clothes,* the key, but we would not add it to the paragraph because it has a different topic,

Charlie | _____. ☐

The two sentences we've just looked at don't belong in the paragraph we're developing because they follow a topic or a key not in the topic sentence.

And when it's really cold, he muffles himself in an old black overcoat with a picture of Snoopy painted crudely on the back.

We can add this sentence, however, because it follows both the

key   topic | (topic, key) *odd clothes* and the (topic, key) *George.* ☐

Let's look at another topic sentence we've seen before:

Rats are disease carriers.

rats   disease carriers | The topic is _____. The key is _____. ☐

Rats are disease carriers. **By their presence they can infect whole populations with typhoid fever and bubonic plague, two dread diseases that have killed millions of people.**

The new sentence can follow the topic sentence because it is about rats, the topic, and because *typhoid fever* and *bubonic*

key | *plague* are concrete details of *disease carriers,* the _____. ☐

Rats also destroy food supplies.

We cannot now add this sentence because it does not follow the

key (disease carriers) | (topic, key). ☐

> *The common housefly is a disease carrier.*

We cannot add this sentence either because it does not follow the topic, _____. ☐   *rats*

> *In fact, rats are carriers of a whole spectrum of diseases, from the relatively mild forms of food poisoning to the deadly typhoid fever.*

Can we add this sentence? _____ ☐   *yes*

In both paragraphs we've been developing, the one on George and the one on rats, we've subdivided the keys *(odd clothes, disease carriers)* by supplying concrete details explaining them. Occasionally, we need to subdivide the topic also. To see how this works, let's look again at still another topic sentence we've seen before:

> *What children eat for breakfast can determine how well they function in school.*

The topic of the paragraph is contained in the words *What children eat for breakfast.* The key is contained in the words *how* _____. ☐   *well they function in school*

> *Children who have had an adequate breakfast can most often work up to their capacity.*

In adding this sentence to the topic sentence, we have done two things: first, we have subdivided the topic. Now, instead of dealing with all children's breakfasts, we are dealing with only the breakfasts of those children _____   *who have had an adequate*

_____. ☐   *breakfast.*

> *Children who have had an adequate breakfast,* since it deals with fewer children and in a more specific way, is (more, less)   *more*
> concrete than the topic, *what children eat for breakfast.* ☐

Children who have had an adequate breakfast can most often work up to their capacity.

Notice that we have also subdivided the key. *To their capacity* is (more, less) concrete than the key *how well they function in school.* ☐

more

In contrast, children who begin their day without adequate nourishment, because of poverty or ignorance, will tend to be listless, unable to respond to the tasks of learning.

In adding this sentence, we have done the same—subdivided the topic and key. *Children who begin their day without adequate nourishment,* like *Children who have had an adequate breakfast,* is another subdivision of the topic and is more (concrete, abstract). ☐

concrete

Listless, unable to respond to the tasks of learning, like *to their capacity,* is another subdivision of the key *how well they function in school* and is more (concrete, abstract). ☐

concrete

Children who have sympathetic teachers usually perform well in school.

We would not add this sentence because it does not follow (the topic, the key, either topic or key). ☐

the topic

Children who are adequately nourished normally make friends more easily than those who are not.

We would not add this sentence because it does not follow (the topic, the key, either topic or key). ☐

the key

When they are adequately nourished, slow learners whose difficulty is lack of a decent diet can surprise their teachers by performing far above their usual low level.

Can we add this sentence? _____ ☐

yes

Here is another topic sentence, one we haven't dealt with before:

Trying to get something from coin-operated machines can be maddening.

The topic is contained in the whole phrase which ends with the word _____. The key is contained in one word, _____. □

machines

maddening

In the next frames we'll add sentences to this topic sentence and develop the paragraph. Indicate after each addition whether or not the sentence belongs.

Trying to get something from coin-operated machines can be maddening. **Some machines, born criminals, gulp your coin and drop nothing into your expectant hand.**

Be sure to check all necessary parts of the response.

( )   Yes, we can add this sentence.

( )   No, we can't, because it does not follow

    ( )   the topic

    ( )   the key

    ( )   either topic or key □

Yes, we can add this sentence.

Trying to get something from coin-operated machines can be maddening. Some machines, born criminals, gulp your coin and drop nothing into your expectant hand. **Some machines, however, work perfectly.**

( )   Yes, we can add this sentence.

( )   No, we can't, because it does not follow

    ( )   the topic

    ( )   the key

    ( )   either topic or key □

No, we can't, because it does not follow the key.

Trying to get something from coin-operated machines can be maddening. Some machines, born criminals, gulp your coin and drop nothing into your expectant hand. **Other machines, with the souls of jokesters, give you a cup with ice but no soda, or they give you ice and soda but skip the cup.**

( )   Yes, we can add this sentence.

( )   No, we can't, because it does not follow

    ( )   the topic

    ( )   the key

    ( )   either topic or key ☐

Yes, we can add this sentence

Trying to get something from coin-operated machines can be maddening. Some machines, born criminals, gulp your coin and drop nothing into your expectant hand. Other machines, with the souls of jokesters, give you a cup with ice but no soda, or they give you ice and soda but skip the cup. **Trying to get service in a large restaurant can be equally maddening.**

( )   Yes, we can add this sentence.

( )   No, we can't, because it does not follow

    ( )   the topic

    ( )   the key

    ( )   either topic or key ☐

No, we can't, because it does not follow the topic.

Trying to get something from coin-operated machines can be maddening. Some machines, born criminals, gulp your coin and drop nothing into your expectant hand. Other machines, with the souls of jokesters, give you a cup with ice but no soda, or they give you ice and soda but skip the cup. **Still others, mysteriously choosy about the kinds of coins they accept, will reject eight dimes you offer them only to accept the ninth.**

( )   Yes, we can add this sentence.

( )   No, we can't, because it does not follow

    ( )   the topic

    ( )   the key

    ( )   either topic or key ☐

Yes, we can add this sentence.

Let's develop another topic sentence in the same way.

Airlines are in deep financial trouble, according to the most recent information.

The topic of the paragraph is expressed in one word,

_____. The key is expressed in three words,

_____. □

Airlines are in deep financial trouble, according to the most recent information. **Airplane manufacturers are having serious financial difficulties of their own.**

( )   Yes, we can add this sentence.

( )   No, we can't, because it does not follow

    ( )   the topic

    ( )   the key

    ( )   either topic or key □

Airlines are in deep financial trouble, according to the most recent information. **Flights the airlines are obliged by law to make often lose money because there are too few passengers aboard.**

( )   Yes, we can add this sentence.

( )   No, we can't, because it does not follow

    ( )   the topic

    ( )   the key

    ( )   either topic or key □

Airlines are in deep financial trouble, according to the most recent information. Flights the airlines are obliged by law to make often lose money because there are too few passengers aboard. **Costly efforts by the airlines to attract more passengers by advertising simply have not worked.**

( )   Yes, we can add this sentence.

( )   No, we can't, because it does not follow

    ( )   the topic

    ( )   the key

    ( )   either topic or key □

Airlines are in deep financial trouble, according to the most recent information. Flights that airlines are obliged by law to make often lose money because there are too few passengers aboard. Costly efforts by the airlines to attract more passengers by advertising simply have not worked. **Airport facilities are larger and more complex than ever before.**

( )   Yes, we can add this sentence.

( )   No, we can't, because it does not follow

      ( )   the topic

      ( )   the key

      ( )   either topic or key □

No, we can't, because it does not follow either topic or key.

Airlines are in deep financial trouble, according to the most recent information. Flights that airlines are obliged by law to make often lose money because there are too few passengers aboard. Costly efforts by the airlines to attract more passengers by advertising simply have not worked. **And at a time when fewer passengers are buying tickets, airline maintenance costs, salaries, and the prices of new equipment are rising steeply.**

( )   Yes, we can add this sentence.

( )   No, we can't, because it does not follow

      ( )   the topic

      ( )   the key

      ( )   either topic or key □

Yes, we can add this sentence.

There is another kind of sentence we often add to paragraphs, one that does not specifically follow both topic and key. To see what we mean, let's go back to the paragraph about George and his odd clothes.

George wears odd clothes. In most weather he wears a pair of striped coveralls cut off at the knees. **Once black and white, the stripes are now two shades of gray.**

Notice what the sentence added here does: it gives some more concrete information about one small detail in the sentence it comes after, the _____ of the coveralls. □

stripes

George wears odd clothes. In most weather he wears a pair
of striped coveralls cut off at the knees. **Once black and**
white, the stripes are now two shades of gray.
We can add sentences to a paragraph if they give more information about a part of another sentence. Therefore, we (can,
cannot) add this sentence. □

can

Compare the sentence we added in the last frame with one we
rejected earlier:

Charlie, George's friend, also wears odd clothes.
Remember, we said we would not add this sentence to the paragraph because it introduces a new (topic, key), *Charlie.* □

topic

George drives a red and yellow striped Volkswagen.
We also rejected this sentence because it introduces a new
(topic, key), *a red and yellow striped Volkswagen.* □

key

We can add sentences to a paragraph if they give more information about part of a sentence in the paragraph, provided they do
not introduce a new topic or key.

Trying to get something from coin-operated machines can be
maddening. Some machines, born criminals, gulp your coin
and drop nothing into your expectant hand. **Punches and**
kicks won't make these machines cough up the stolen coin.
Here's part of another paragraph we've already developed. Can
we add the new sentence? □

yes

Airlines are in deep financial trouble, according to the most
recent information. Flights the airlines are obliged by law to
make often lose money because there are too few passengers
aboard.

Such money-losing flights are all too common on both
domestic and overseas routes.

Airline passengers have been pampered more than any other
group of travelers.
Only one of these sentences gives added information and does not
introduce a new topic or key. Therefore, we can add only the
(first, second) sentence to the paragraph. □

first

Most of the sentences we add to the topic sentence in developing a paragraph will follow both topic and key. Others will give more information about a part of sentences they follow. But no sentence in a well-developed paragraph will introduce a new topic or key.

The almost-forgotten art of sewing has become popular among the younger generation of women.

Here is a new topic sentence. *The almost-forgotten art of sewing* is the (topic, key), and *popular among the younger generation of women* is the (topic, key). □

The almost-forgotten art of sewing has become popular among the younger generation of women.

Many girls whose mothers never learned to sew are spending a large part of their clothing budget on sewing machines, patterns, and material instead of ready-to-wear clothes.

The sewing machines now on the market are much more versatile and complex than earlier models.

We can add only one of these new sentences, the (first, second), because it (follows topic and key, gives information about part of the sentence before). □

The almost-forgotten art of sewing has become popular among the younger generation of women. Girls whose mothers never learned to sew are spending a large part of their clothing budget on sewing machines, patterns, and material instead of ready-to-wear clothes.

The high cost of clothes can stretch a young girl's budget to the breaking point.

Clothing manufacturers spend a great deal of money and effort creating new styles.

We can add only one of these sentences, the (first, second), because it (follows topic and key, gives information about part of the sentence before). □

topic
key

first
follows topic and key

first
gives information about part of
the sentence before

The almost-forgotten art of sewing has become popular among the younger generation of women. Many girls whose mothers never learned to sew are spending a large part of their clothing budget on sewing machines, patterns, and material instead of ready-to-wear clothes. The high cost of clothes can stretch a young girl's budget to the breaking point.

But some women, young or old, simply don't care for sewing because it's much easier, and often just as cheap, to buy ready-made clothes.

But there is more than the cost of ready-to-wear clothes involved in the popularity of sewing; for the young dress-maker there is pride of accomplishment and freedom to add personal touches that simply buying clothes does not offer.

We can add only one of these sentences, the (first, second), because it (follows topic and key, gives information about part of the sentence before). ☐

second

follows topic and key

So far we have assumed that the topic sentence is the first sentence in a paragraph. In almost all cases, that's the best place for it because it gives the reader a base to put together in his mind the ideas in the sentences that follow. Keep in mind that the topic sentence is always the most (general, particular) statement in the paragraph. ☐

general

The topic sentence is the most general statement in the paragraph because it contains at least one word or phrase more (concrete, abstract) than related words or phrases in the sentences that follow. ☐

abstract

For special effect we can sometimes move the topic sentence to other positions in a paragraph, particularly to the end of the paragraph. To see the effect, let's develop a paragraph and place the topic sentence last.

Bob is car-crazy.

Bob | Here's a very simple topic sentence. The topic is _____,
car-crazy | the key is _____. □

Instead of putting the topic sentence first we'll keep it in the front of our mind and begin the paragraph with one of the more particular statements related to it.

Bob reads every magazine and book about cars he can get his hands on.

Bob is fond of everything that has a motor in it.

Though we do not begin with the topic sentence, it will be our base. Only one of these sentences follows the topic and key,
first | the (first, second). □

Bob reads every magazine and book about cars he can get his hands on.

He went out for football last year, but because of his light weight, he was cut from the team.

He spends endless hours talking about cars to everyone who will listen.

second | We can add only one of these sentences, the (first, second). □

Bob reads every magazine and book about cars he can get his hands on. He spends endless hours talking about cars to anyone who will listen.

Every penny he can scrape up goes for gas and oil and parts to keep his ancient Ford running smoothly.

He is not very thrifty and often spends his entire allowance on things he doesn't really need.

first | We can add only one of these sentences, the (first, second). □

We can now add the topic sentence.

Bob reads every magazine and book about cars he can get his hands on. He spends endless hours talking about cars to anyone who will listen. Every penny he can scrape up goes for gas and oil and parts to keep his ancient Ford running smoothly. In short, _____. ☐ | *Bob is car-crazy.*

Notice that we have expanded the original topic sentence by adding a signal to the reader that the sentence is a more general statement than the other sentences in the paragraph. That two-word signal is _____. ☐ | *In short*

It is often helpful to add such signals when we put the topic sentence last. Others like it are *therefore, thus, so,* and *consequently.* If we put the topic sentence first—which we could—the signal *In short* (would, would not) be necessary. ☐ | *would not*

Putting the topic sentence last can have an effect like that of the punch line of a joke—humorous surprise. However, we can put the topic sentence last for more serious reasons, such as showing the reader the particular events or ideas that lead us to conclude what we do in the general statement.

A child's experience provides his earliest instruction on the basic facts of life.

Here is a more complicated topic sentence. *A child's experience* is the (topic, key); *his earliest instruction on the basic facts of life* is the (topic, key). ☐ | *topic* / *key*

Once again, we'll save the topic sentence until the end, but we'll choose the sentences for the paragraph with topic and key firmly in mind.

A child who minds his parents can often escape the painful experience of being burned by some hot object.

A child is not born knowing that hot objects will burn him but must learn that fact by the painful experience of being burned.

Be careful: only one of these sentences follows both topic and key, the (first, second). ☐ | *second*

A child is not born knowing that hot objects will burn him but must learn that fact by the painful experience of being burned.

Similarly he must learn that sharp objects will cut him and make him bleed by being cut.

A child will often be afraid of water if he is not exposed to the new element carefully.

Only one of these new sentences follows both topic and key, the *first* (first, second). ☐

A child is not born knowing that hot objects will burn him but must learn that fact by the painful experience of being burned. Similarly, he must learn that sharp objects will cut him and make him bleed by being cut.

Repeated experience also teaches a child that people do not grow smaller when they walk away and seem smaller to him.

A child is much more determined than any adult when he undertakes such exacting tasks as learning to walk.

Only one of these sentences follows both topic and key, the *first* (first, second). ☐

A child is not born knowing that hot objects will burn him but must learn that fact by the painful experience of being burned. Similarly, he must learn that sharp objects will cut him and make him bleed by being cut. Repeated experience also teaches a child that people do not grow smaller when they walk away and seem smaller to him.

A child can spend hours amusing himself by playing with his own image in a mirror.

A child's experiments in front of a mirror, often comic, show him that the image is himself and not some other child.

Only one of these sentences follows topic and key, the (first, *second* second). ☐

A child is not born knowing that hot objects will burn him but must learn that fact by the painful experience of being burned. Similarly, he must learn that sharp objects will cut him and make him bleed by being cut. Repeated experience also teaches a child that people do not grow smaller when they walk away and seem smaller to him. A child's experiments in front of a mirror, often comic, show him that the image is himself and not some other child.

Now we can add the topic sentence, introducing it with a signal such as *Thus:*

_____, _____

_____

_____ . ☐

Thus, a child's experience provides his earliest instruction on the basic facts of life.

PARAGRAPH COHERENCE

Now that you know how to add sentences to a topic sentence to form a paragraph, we can look at the devices writers use to give paragraphs the coherence they need. Coherence means *sticking together:* all the sentences of a paragraph should stick together in a way that allows the reader to see immediately how each sentence connects to the others. Giving a paragraph coherence is simply a matter of using in a commonsense way the signals that guide the reader from one sentence to another.

To avoid the awkward repetition of words and phrases in related sentences, we will often use synonyms—words and phrases that have the same meaning as other words and phrases.

> *Joe was well aware of the manager's intention to move him to the Chicago office. He knew that the senior accountant's job was open there and that he was the obvious choice.*

In the second sentence here we have used a synonym for *was . . . aware* in the first sentence, _____. ☐

knew

> *Joe was well aware of the manager's intention to move him to the Chicago office. He knew that the senior accountant's job was open there and that he was the obvious choice.*

The second sentence has another synonym. Instead of repeating *Chicago,* we have simply used the word _____. ☐

there

> *The noise was intense. Sounds of rivet guns and power saws filled our ears.*

Sounds in the second sentence is a _____ for *noise* in the first. ☐

synonym

Using synonyms, particularly if sentences are short, can help us avoid monotony.

> *It was an emotional moment for Roy. His (emotions, feelings) were all on the side of the young boy the other children were teasing.*

To avoid the monotony of repetition, the better choice is *(emotions, feelings).* ☐

feelings

A magnetic compass will be useless if the case becomes bent
so that the needle cannot swing freely. (A magnetic compass,
Such an instrument) should be carefully protected at all times.
Choose the better completion for this sentence. ☐   *Such an instrument*

The Great Depression began with the stock market crash
in 1929 and lasted almost without relief for ten years.
During (the ten years, this period) most of the nations of
this hemisphere and Western Europe suffered severe hardship.
Choose the better completion for this sentence. ☐   *this period*

When words or phrases with the same meaning in two related
sentences are far apart, it is better usually to repeat the word
or part of the phrase. In such cases the repetition will not be
monotonous, and it will help link sentences together, particularly
when they are long.

The process of firing clay in a kiln is extremely exacting
because a constant temperature is necessary. No one should
begin this (process, work) unless he fully understands use of
the equipment.
The better choice for completing the second sentence so that it
will be clearly related to the first is _____. ☐   *process*

All kinds of well-engineered and well-made electronic
equipment from Japan have flooded the American market
during recent years, often outselling the equivalent domestic
products by a considerable margin. This _____
is almost always quite imaginatively designed.
The best choice to complete the second sentence in a way that
links it to the first is a single word in the first, _____. ☐   *equipment*

The political and social unrest afflicting so many college
campuses during recent years may seem to the outsider to
have died down lately. Those who are close to the campuses,
however, know that this _____ has simply taken   *unrest*
new and more subtle forms.
Complete the second sentence so that it is linked to the first. ☐

Do the same with these sentences:

Beauty pageants, particularly those covered by television, appear to have become permanent fixtures, gaining rather than losing audiences over the years. What some people don't realize is that such _____ are big business for those who produce them. ☐

pageants

Another important way we signal the connection between related sentences is with traditional words and phrases. To keep our language simple, we'll call them simply "linkers."

Some experts have predicted that the population explosion will soon make human life intolerable, if not impossible. However, other experts, equally well qualified, have challenged that conclusion.

These two sentences are joined by a word that signals how their ideas are related, _____. ☐

However

However is one of several linkers that signal the connection between sentences having contrasting ideas. Others with the same meaning are *nevertheless, nonetheless* (formal), *yet, still,* and *but* (less formal).

A good deal of enthusiasm has sprung up nationally for including sex education in the curriculums of public schools. There is, nevertheless, strong opposition to the idea.

Although it does not come between them, the linker showing how these sentences are related is _____. ☐

nevertheless

Some linkers can move about freely in a sentence. Others cannot, but must be the first word.

There is, nevertheless, strong opposition to the idea.

We can replace *nevertheless* with *however* in this sentence. Can we replace it with *but?* _____ ☐

no

Though a linker may come first, somewhere in the middle, or last in a sentence, it always links that sentence to the one coming before it.

> *New York City is a hard three-day trip by car from Kansas City. Yet by plane, it is only three hours away.*

The linker signaling that the second sentence expresses an idea contrasted to the idea of the first is _____. ☐   *Yet*

When two sentences expressing contrasting ideas are very short, the contrast will be obvious and no linker is needed.

> *Some people like Mexican food. Others don't.*

Would *however* or one of the other linkers signaling contrast be necessary in the second sentence? _____ ☐   *no*

When related sentences expressing a contrast are not very short, a linker helps the reader see their relationship at a glance.

> *Most of Minnesota's 10,000 lakes are startlingly pure and clear, making them ideal for all kinds of water sports. A few of them near large cities are polluted.*

A linker like *but* or *however* signaling a contrast (would, would not) be necessary here. ☐   *would*

Phrases as well as single words act as linkers signaling contrast: *on the other hand, on the contrary, in contrast* are the most familiar. But they do not have precisely the same meaning as *however* and other one-word linkers.

> *The colors in the early Technicolor movies tended to be gaudy and unnatural. _____, the Technicolor movies made recently have very lifelike colors.*

Only one of the phrases above can link these sentences,

_____. ☐   *In contrast*

> *John Wayne has made scores of movies in which he has appeared in he-man roles. The only time we see him not in a military uniform is when he is on horseback chasing cattle rustlers across the prairie.*

> *Bloodstains, once set, are extremely difficult to remove from clothing. If the clothing is rinsed before such stains set, they wash out easily.*

Only one of these pairs needs a linker signaling contrast, the

second | (first, second). ☐

Another important group of linkers are those signaling that a sentence following another expresses a similar idea: *furthermore, moreover* (formal), *similarly, also, in addition* (less formal).

> *The school board voted last night to increase funds available to programs for exceptional children. In addition, they agreed to increase the number of staff positions for such programs.*

In addition signals that the ideas expressed in the second sen-

similar | tence are _____ to those expressed in the first. ☐

Be sure you choose the linker that signals the true relationship between sentences.

> *He had lost the slip of paper he had written her phone number on. (However, Also), he had forgotten her address.*

similar | Since these two sentences express (similar, contrasting) ideas,

Also | the linker needed is *(However, Also)*. ☐

> *The older parts of downtown Los Angeles have become almost unbelievably run-down slums, with crime of every kind a regular occurrence. (Yet, Moreover), large numbers of people find it somehow possible to live and work in these appalling surroundings.*

contrasting | Since these two sentences express (similar, contrasting) ideas,

Yet | the linker needed is *(Yet, Moreover)*. ☐

> *The many pack trails in the Colorado Rockies make it possible*
> *for the inexperienced hiker to find his way into the wilder-*
> *ness—and out again—without difficulty or danger. (However,*
> *Similarly), access trails to the very top of many of the*
> *fourteen-thousand-foot peaks make mountain climbing fairly*
> *easy even for someone lacking the mountain climber's technical*
> *skills.*

Since these two sentences express (similar, contrasting) ideas, the linker needed is *(However, Similarly).* ☐

Still another group of linkers signal a conclusion: *in conclusion, consequently* (formal), *therefore, in short, thus, so* (less formal).

> *Some students traveling to Europe during the summer months*
> *have been stranded there when the companies managing their*
> *tours have gone bankrupt and failed to meet their obligations*
> *to return them to the United States. Thus, a student planning*
> *a trip to Europe would do well to choose carefully what*
> *company he schedules his tour with.*

Thus is the right linker here because the second sentence is a _____ following from the first. ☐

> *Few, if any, movements have struck so many sparks among so*
> *many people so fast as the women's liberation movement.*
> *It would seem, therefore, that the issues raised by the*
> *movement's leaders have existed under the surface for a long*
> *time.*

Though it does not come first in the sentence, the linker showing that the second sentence is a conclusion following from the first is _____. ☐

The linkers we have seen so far signal contrast, similarity, or conclusion. Choose the right completion for the second sentence:

> *Ex-servicemen are beginning to take advantage of the*
> *educational opportunities offered them under the GI Bill of*
> *Rights. (But, Also, So) fewer of them are in college now*
> *than ex-servicemen following World War II.* ☐

Choose the right completion for the second sentence:

> *Since parts for most antique cars are no longer available,*
> *their owners must make them or have them made by a*
> *specialist. (Consequently, In contrast, In addition), owners*
> *must be able to do their own repair work if they do not have*
> *the services of the rare mechanic who knows enough to do*
> *the work for them.* ☐

In addition

Choose the right completion for the second sentence:

> *People trained as computer programmers are in high demand*
> *even at a time when other specialists such as draftsmen*
> *and bookkeepers are having difficulty finding and keeping*
> *work. (On the other hand, Therefore, Furthermore), pro-*
> *grammers can count on greater job security than other*
> *specialists equally well trained.* ☐

Therefore

When we add a sentence containing an example or a particular instance of something we are writing about, it is often helpful to include a linker such as *in particular, for example,* or *for instance.*

> *Not all trees are the good guys in our environment, changing*
> *carbon dioxide into oxygen we can breathe. Eucalyptus trees*
> *give off chemicals as dangerous to health as automobile*
> *exhausts.*

It would help to add a linker, *for instance* or *for example,* to the second sentence because it contains an _____ of the idea expressed in the first sentence. ☐

example (instance)

Complete the second sentence with a helpful linker:

> *A good many of the well-meaning men who manage Little*
> *League teams are guilty of stressing the wrong values in*
> *dealing with their young players. _____,*
> *their tendency to exaggerate the value of winning can do*
> *serious psychological harm.* ☐

In particular would be the best choice here, but *for example* or *for instance* will do.

Now we have looked at four kinds of linkers, those signaling contrast, similarity, conclusion, and example. Choose the best linker for the second sentence:

> *Transistors, invented thirty years ago, have made formerly impossible or extremely difficult scientific achievements possible and even easy. (Therefore, For instance), without transistors, flight to the moon would have been impossible.* □

For instance

Choose the best linker for the second sentence:

> *Politicians at all levels—local, state, and national—will sometimes promise almost anything to get themselves elected. (In particular, Thus) those who promise too much should not be surprised when criticized for failing to keep promises they never intended to keep.* □

Thus

The last group of linkers we'll look at are the simplest—those that signal divisions: *to begin with, first, second (secondly), next, third (thirdly), then, finally, last (lastly).* When dividing our ideas into stages or steps, these linkers help the reader see where one stage or step leaves off and another begins.

> *Removing a wheel from a car is easy if you have the tools and the energy. First, jack up the car until the tire clears the ground. Second, remove the hubcap. Third, remove the five nuts or lug bolts with the lug wrench. Then slide the wheel off.*

Identify all the linkers in this paragraph. □

First   Second   Third   Then

Add the linkers to these sentences:

> *Our trip to Phoenix was a near disaster. _____, we were late to the airport, so we missed our flight and had to go on a later one. _____, our luggage was routed to Dallas and had to be sent to our hotel the next day. And _____, our room reservation had been lost, and we spent the first night in a run-down hotel right on Skid Row.* □

First (To begin with)

Then (Next, Second)

finally (then, third, last)

REVIEW: PARAGRAPHS

In this and the following two frames, number the statements from the most general to the most particular:

( ) *Cigarettes are dangerous because they contain harmful tars and nicotine.*

( ) *Gaspers, a leading brand, has the highest tar and nicotine content of any cigarette.*

( ) *Some cigarettes contain more tars and nicotine than others.* □

1, 3, 2

( ) *For instance, a group of teen-agers in our neighborhood have set up a dog-bathing service, sparing the owner the unpleasant task for a modest fee.*

( ) *Some are quite imaginative, making jobs for themselves in surprising ways.*

( ) *Many young people manage somehow to find summer employment.* □

3, 2, 1

( ) *One excellent book on making violins is Leroy Geiger's* How to Make Your Own Violin.

( ) *There are do-it-yourself books on almost every conceivable project, from jar collecting to making paper flowers.*

( ) *Books are a useful starting point for anyone interested in a do-it-yourself project.*

( ) *For instance, several fine books on how to make and repair violins are available to anyone interested in these exacting skills.* □

4, 2, 1, 3

Identify and label the topic and key in the following topic sentences:

1. *Flying an airplane is an exciting sport.*

2. *Society in the United States seems to be undergoing a major cultural change.*

3. *One-quarter of all marriages end in divorce, research has shown.*

4. *Broken Arrow Grammar School is divided into four large areas called "colonies."* ☐

1. Topic: *Flying an airplane;* key: *an exciting sport*
2. Topic: *Society in the United States;* key: *a major cultural change*
3. Topic: *One-quarter of all marriages;* key: *divorce*
4. Topic: *Broken Arrow Grammar School;* key: *four large areas called "colonies"*

Babe Ruth still holds (an important baseball record, the all-time home run record).
Choose the better key for the topic sentence of a paragraph on Babe Ruth's record as a batter. ☐

the all-time home run record

Young adults, when they marry, tend to become (quite a bit different, members of the Republican Party, as conservative as their parents).
Choose the best key for the topic sentence of a paragraph on the tendency of young married people to become less radical or liberal. ☐

as conservative as their parents

Efforts to hold the wage-price spiral within reasonable limits have had (no success, interesting results, success in keeping down the price of haircuts).
Choose the best key for the topic sentence of a paragraph on the failure of efforts to slow down inflation. ☐

no success

George's car is his worst enemy.
The topic of a paragraph this topic sentence introduces will be
_____. The key will be
_____. ☐

George's car

his worst enemy

George's car is his worst enemy. **When it runs out of gas, as it often does, it is usually on the inside lane of the San Diego Freeway, with the gas gauge deceptively showing half-full.**

( ) We can add this sentence because it

    ( ) follows topic and key

    ( ) gives information about part of the sentence before

( ) We can't add this sentence because it does not follow

    ( ) the topic

    ( ) the key

    ( ) either topic or key ☐

We can add this sentence because it follows topic and key.

George's car is his worst enemy. When it runs out of gas, as it often does, it is usually on the inside lane of the San Diego Freeway, with the gas gauge deceptively showing half-full. **Usually, though, the car provides George with a handy means of transportation.**

( ) We can add this sentence because it

    ( ) follows topic and key

    ( ) gives information about part of the sentence before

( ) We can't add this sentence because it does not follow

    ( ) the topic

    ( ) the key

    ( ) either topic or key ☐

We can't add this sentence because it does not follow the key.

George's car is his worst enemy. When it runs out of gas, as it often does, it is usually on the inside lane of the San Diego Freeway, with the gas gauge deceptively showing half-full. **It seldom has a flat tire—except when it rains.**

( ) We can add this sentence because it

    ( ) follows topic and key

    ( ) gives information about part of the sentence before

( ) We can't add this sentence because it does not follow

    ( ) the topic

    ( ) the key

    ( ) either topic or key □

We can add this sentence because it follows topic and key.

George's car is his worse enemy. When it runs out of gas, as it often does, it is usually on the inside lane of the San Diego Freeway, with the gas gauge deceptively showing half-full. It seldom has a flat tire—except when it rains. **George's father has exactly the same make and model of car, but his is twenty years younger than George's.**

( ) We can add this sentence because it

    ( ) follows topic and key

    ( ) gives information about part of the sentence before

( ) We can't add this sentence because it does not follow

    ( ) the topic

    ( ) the key

    ( ) either topic or key □

We can't add this sentence because it does not follow the key.

George's car is his worst enemy. When it runs out of gas, as it often does, it is usually on the inside lane of the San Diego Freeway, with the gas gauge deceptively showing half-full. It seldom has a flat tire—except when it rains. **It will not start on cold mornings, or on warm mornings without a push.**

( ) We can add this sentence because it

    ( ) follows topic and key

    ( ) adds information about part of the sentence before

( ) We can't add this sentence because it does not follow

    ( ) the topic

    ( ) the key

    ( ) either topic or key □

We can add this sentence because it follows topic and key.

George's car is his worst enemy. When it runs out of gas, as it often does, it is usually on the inside lane of the San Diego Freeway, with the gas gauge deceptively showing half-full. It seldom has a flat tire—except when it rains. It will not start on cold mornings, or on warm mornings without a push. **George's motorcycle is, if anything, in worse shape than his car.**

( ) We can add this sentence because it

    ( ) follows topic and key

    ( ) adds information about part of the sentence before

( ) We can't add this sentence because it does not follow

    ( ) the topic

    ( ) the key

    ( ) either topic or key □

We can't add this sentence because it does not follow the topic.

*George's car is his worst enemy. When it runs out of gas,
as it often does, it is usually on the inside lane of the San
Diego Freeway, with the gas gauge deceptively showing half-
full. It seldom has a flat tire—except when it rains. It will
not start on cold mornings, or on warm mornings without
a push.* **When George finally took his father's advice and
tried to sell it for junk, he discovered that it would cost
more than he could afford to have it towed away.**

( )   We can add this sentence because it

      ( )   follows topic and key

      ( )   adds information about part of the sentence
            before

( )   We can't add this sentence because it does not follow

      ( )   the topic

      ( )   the key

      ( )   either topic or key ☐

*We can add this sentence because
it follows topic and key.*

*Anyone familiar with science knows that there are several
theories about the origin of the universe, each one having
numerous advocates. Because they are based on different uses
of the scientific data, these (ideas about the origin of the
universe, theories) tend to be contradictory.*

Choose the completion for the second sentence that links both
sentences more closely together. ☐

theories

*Between the mountains that rim the coast of California
and the Sierra Nevada Mountains that border it on the east
lies the San Joaquin Valley. Because of the rich soil and
the mild winter climate, this (valley, tract of land) contains
some of the most productive farms in the world.*

Choose the completion for the second sentence that links both
sentences more closely together. ☐

valley

Choose the right linker for the second sentence:

Thus

> *An old refrigerator can make an attractive hiding place for young children—and become a death trap. (Thus, However), most cities have ordinances requiring owners to remove the doors of refrigerators not in use.* □

Choose the right linker for the second sentence:

On the other hand

> *The people in Calcutta live for the most part in conditions that appall the American visitor with the signs of poverty and disease. (On the other hand, Moreover), some people in Calcutta are very wealthy and live comfortably somehow apart from the general misery.* □

Choose the right linker for the second sentence:

For example

> *Almost all my friends seem to have at least one peculiar habit. (Similarly, For example), Bob Allen, someone I've known for years, always tugs at the lobe of one of his ears when he talks.* □

FOUR
THE WHOLE ESSAY

Writing needs purpose. Before we begin any kind of writing assignment, we must know what we are going to write about—a subject—and what we are going to say about that subject. In Part Four we will work with the problems of choosing a subject and deciding on our treatment of it. At the end we will put together an entire essay from start to finish, using all the skills covered in this text.

FINDING A SUBJECT

Anything can be the subject of a writing assignment—anything from nuclear warfare to the fine art of throwing a frisbee. But of course no one can write equally well about most subjects. High school seniors and college freshmen can't expect to write about the more technical sides of physics or psychology. For instance, an essay on the design of nuclear reactors for power generators (would, would not) be beyond their capabilities. □

would

Some subjects are too complex for a high school senior or college freshman to tackle. Others are too simple—picking a daisy, Aunt Maud's bifocals. But between the too-complex and too-simple is a whole range of subjects that a student, with or without a little research, can handle.

1. *Local campus radicalism*
2. *The art of haiku poetry*
3. *The college sky diving club*
4. *Fraternities and sororities*
5. *Binary computers*

2, 5   Only two of these subjects would be beyond the powers of most young students, numbers _____ and _____ . □

We can write best about what we know best. When you have a choice, as you often do, you should certainly pick a subject that you already know something about—and if necessary get additional information about it from books or magazines or a local expert. The best place to look for a subject, then, is your own experience. For instance, what are your hobbies?

Any response, if it satisfies you,   _____   _____

is right.   _____   _____ □

Beyond your hobbies, you probably have special interests—politics, astrology, religion, native birds of North America. What are yours?

Once again, any response that   _____   _____

satisfies you is right.   _____   _____ □

A hobby or special interest is the best kind of subject because we already know enough about it not to need much additional information. But having chosen our subject, we've only begun the job. What we must do next is limit the subject to manageable proportions. For instance, suppose you said that sports is one of your special interests. Volumes have been written on the subject, so as it stands the subject *sports* is too (broad, limited) for the kind of short essay students generally write. □

broad

Having chosen our subject, we need to reduce it to manageable limits. What sports are you interested in—football, track, hockey? And what kind of football—professional, college, high school? Or are you interested in some special feature of football such as line play or quarterbacking? Notice that in asking these questions, we have followed a process we've seen elsewhere in this book: we've gone from the abstract term *sports* to the more (abstract, concrete) terms such as *quarterbacking* and *line play*. □

concrete

To limit our subject, we simply look for more concrete terms. Suppose you had chosen fashions as a special interest. Two terms more concrete than *fashions* are *women's fashions* and _____ *fashions*. □

men's

Though relatively concrete when compared to *fashions* by itself, *women's fashions* and *men's fashions* are probably still too broad for a short paper. *Women's hair styles*, for example, is more (concrete, abstract) than *women's fashions*. □

concrete

But we can still ask the question, "What women's hair styles?" *Women's hair styles of the 1920s* is one possibility. Using a time period, write another more concrete form of *women's hair styles*:

_____

_____ □

New women's hair styles and *women's hair styles of the Gay Nineties* are two possibilities.

Let's go through this limiting process with another subject, *photography*. There are many kinds of photography: *portrait photography* and *landscape photography*, for instance. Name two others:

Baby photography, bird photography, medical photography, industrial photography, pet photography are a few examples.

_____

_____ □

If you have the necessary information, *new women's hair styles* and *baby photography* are probably good subjects for a short paper. Using the process once again, take the general subject *recreation* and limit it until you have a subject as concrete as our examples.

    recreation
    outdoor recreation

Examples: *competitive sports, tennis, competitive tennis in college; boating, power boating, power boating on rivers; motorcycling, off-highway cycling, hill climbing*

_____

_____

_____ □

Let's do one more, this time on the general subject *movies*.

movies

——————————————————————————
——————————————————————————
——————————————————————————
——————————————————————————
———————————————————————— □

Examples: *musicals, Elvis Presley classics, typical plots of Elvis Presley classics;—X-rated movies, Swedish X-rated movies, nudity in Swedish X-rated movies;—foreign films, Japanese films, recent Japanese films about death*

PREPARING A THESIS

Once we choose a subject and reduce it to manageable limits, we still have to decide what we are going to say about it.

>*Good line play in football has two qualities, quickness and power.*

>*Recent meetings of student activist groups on campus*

first | Only one of these shows clearly that the writer knows what he is going to say about his subject, the (first, second). ☐

We know that we have something to say about a subject when we can make it part of a complete sentence.

>*free play for young children*

no | Does this show that the writer has something to say about his subject? _____ ☐

>*Free play for young children is a crucial part of their learning experience.*

(complete) sentence | Now the writer has something to say about his subject because he has made it part of a _____. ☐

Complete the sentence for this subject any way you wish:

>*Recent meetings of student activist groups on campus*

Two examples are *were poorly attended* and *were prohibited by the president.*

_____

_____

_____. ☐

A sentence that includes the subject and expresses what we are going to say about it is called a thesis or a thesis statement. Here, let's use the shorter term. *Recent meetings of student activist groups on campus were prohibited by the president* is an

thesis | example of a _____. ☐

A thesis is like the topic sentence of a paragraph in that it is a general statement covering what follows. And in writing a good thesis, we use the same principles as those for writing a good topic sentence.

Purple martins are interesting birds.

Although a complete sentence, this would not be a good thesis because it is too general. The problem lies in one word that's too abstract, _____. □

interesting

A purple martin can eat 10,000 mosquitoes in a single day.

This sentence would not be a good thesis either because it contains only (abstract, concrete) information. □

concrete

A thesis must be just general enough to cover a writing assignment.

Purple martins travel unusually long distances during their semiannual migrations.

For an essay explaining how purple martins travel from one continent to another, this would be a (good, poor) thesis. □

good

Choose the best completion for a thesis of an essay on the unusually high prices in restaurants near a campus:

A casual survey shows that prices in the restaurants near campus are (noticeably higher than average, remarkable when compared with prices elsewhere, one dollar for a hamburger and fifty cents for a milk shake). □

noticeably higher than average

Making sure the thesis for a writing assignment is just general enough to cover what follows helps reduce the certain frustration of trying to begin writing without having a direction to take. Choose the best completion for a thesis covering the difficulties of becoming a successful actress:

A young woman who wants to be a successful actress faces (the problem of dealing with untrustworthy people; a whole series of different kinds of problems; the need for hard work, for courage, and for more than average luck). □

the need for hard work, for courage, and for more than average luck

Writing a good thesis is not waste motion because we can use it in our first paragraph, often as the topic sentence. Choose the best completion for a thesis on how improved lighting has helped cut down crime in cities:

reduce the number and severity of crimes in the streets

> *Tests have shown that improved lighting can help (cities in an important way, reduce the number and severity of crimes in the streets, chase muggers away).* □

Choose the best completion for a thesis on the necessity of student participation in all decisions affecting a school:

their right to share in decisions affecting their lives

> *The participation of students in school government will allow students (their right to share in decisions affecting their lives, their chance to make changes, their voice in the management of the athletic program among others).* □

SNOWBALLING

Once you have a clear thesis, the next step is to put down on paper, in any order, all the particular statements you want to include in your essay. We say "any order" because that marvelous gadget, the human mind, does not work systematically, much as we sometimes wish it would. Putting down your ideas as they occur to you is the easiest, most natural way to get the raw materials you need to begin with. Only after you have the raw materials can you put them in proper order for the actual writing.

Roll a small snowball down a hill and you know what you get—a big snowball. That's what this process of putting down our ideas as they occur to us is like, so we'll call it "snowballing." Let's see how this works by beginning with a thesis—our small snowball—and letting it pick up ideas as it rolls along.

Thesis: *When buying a bicycle, base your choice on your budget and your transportation needs.*

Some fine ten-speed bikes can cost as much as $300.
Motorcycles are inexpensive to operate.

Suppose that, as you thought about the thesis, these two statements occurred to you. But only one of them has to do with our thesis, the (first, second). ☐

first

A snowball rolling downhill doesn't pick up all the snow on the hillside. Similarly, all the ideas that occur to us when we focus on the thesis may not be directly related to it. We add to our list—our large snowball—only those statements within the range of the thesis.

The heavy balloon-tired bikes that young children like are too heavy for long-distance cycling.
Bicycling is a form of exercise recommended by medical experts.

Be careful: only one of these statements is within the range of the thesis, the (first, second). ☐

first

Keep every item on your list a statement—a complete sentence. Words or phrases aren't much help by themselves because they are only pieces of ideas.

> *a lightweight three-speed bike with hand brakes*
> *Lightweight three-speed bikes are heavier than the*
> *standard ten-speed bikes.*

Only one of these items should be part of our list, the

second (first, second). □

Snowballing is straightforward, uncomplicated: we just focus on the thesis and write complete statements.

> *When buying a bicycle, there are three basic kinds to*
> *consider.*
> *A dozen or so of the local bicycle enthusiasts have*
> *formed a cycling club.*

first Only one of these items fits our list, the (first, second). □

> *Bicycle racing is extremely popular in Europe.*
> *Balloon-tired bikes are usually much less expensive*
> *than any of the lightweight bikes.*

second Only one of these items fits our list, the (first, second). □

For a short essay we would continue until we have ten statements or so on our list. To be sure the process is clear to you, we'll begin with a new thesis and continue until the job is completed.

> Thesis: *Living off campus can be much more economi-*
> *cal than living on campus in a dormitory.*

> *Studying in a dorm is often impossible.*
> *Students living on campus may pay twice as much for*
> *room and board as they need to.*

Only one of these statements is related to our thesis, the

second (first, second). □

Living at home while going to school is usually the most economical arrangement for a student.

Incidental expenses for such necessities as laundry and extra meals can add as much as $500 to the cost of dorm living.

(The first, The second, Both, Neither) statement(s) should be on our list. ☐ — *Both*

Apartments, though expensive, can be shared comfortably by a group of students for as little as $35 a month rent.

In an apartment, a student can keep his own hours.

(The first, The second, Both, Neither) statement(s) should be on our list. ☐ — *The first*

When living together in an apartment, students should share the housekeeping responsibilities equally to avoid friction.

Room and board at a dorm costs $1,000 for the two semesters.

(The first, The second, Both, Neither) statement(s) should be on our list. ☐ — *The second*

If a student owns a car, he can come and go as he wishes.

The cost of textbooks has risen more than a third in the last two years.

(The first, The second, Both, Neither) statement(s) should be on our list. ☐ — *Neither*

Room and board costs make the difference in the cost of education because the rest of the charges for education are the same for students living on or off campus.

Cars are too expensive for most students who are self-supporting.

(The first, The second, Both, Neither) statement(s) should be on our list. ☐ — *The first*

When living at home, students whose parents can afford it often do not pay room and board.

When living at home, a student can be close to his neighborhood friends.

The first | (The first, The second, Both, Neither) statement(s) should be on our list. ☐

Fraternities and sororities offer a student the opportunity to make lasting friends, an opportunity not always available to those who live in dorms.

A student living in an apartment can buy enough food for himself for less than $25 a month, if he is careful when shopping.

The second | (The first, The second, Both, Neither) statement(s) should be on our list. ☐

If his family lets a student live at home, even his incidental expenses will be lower.

Dating is a major expense for both men and women students, whether paying for the entertainment or buying clothes—or both.

The first | (The first, The second, Both, Neither) statement(s) should be on our list. ☐

A careful student can live for less than $80 a month in a shared apartment.

Transportation to and from school can be frustrating and time-consuming.

The first | (The first, The second, Both, Neither) statement(s) should be on our list. ☐

OUTLINING

Once you have a list of statements related to your thesis, the next step, and the last before beginning the actual writing, is to organize the statements into a rough working outline. We're not talking here about the formal outline you've seen in writing texts, with neat divisions, subdivisions, and sub-subdivisions. You've probably at some time had to prepare such an outline and discovered how frustrating a job it can be. Here we're talking only about the kind of outline that we can use while actually writing, the kind that makes the writing almost easy if we've done our preliminary work well.

In the last section we made a random list of ten statements, all of them related to this thesis: *Living off campus can be much more economical than living on campus in a dormitory.* Here's the list:

1. *Students living on campus may pay twice as much for room and board as they need to.*

2. *Living at home while going to school is usually the most economical arrangement for a student.*

3. *Incidental expenses for such necessities as laundry and extra meals can add as much as $500 to the cost of dorm living.*

4. *Apartments, though expensive, can be shared comfortably by a group of students for as little as $35 a month rent.*

5. *Room and board at a dorm costs $1,000 for the two semesters.*

6. *Room and board costs make the difference in the cost of education because the rest of the charges for education are the same for students living on or off campus.*

7. *When living at home, students whose parents can afford it often do not pay room and board.*

8. *A student living in an apartment can buy enough food for himself for less than $25 a month, if he is careful when shopping.*

9. *If his family lets a student live at home, even his incidental expenses will be lower.*

10. *A careful student can live for less than $80 a month in a shared apartment.*

When making the kind of working outline we are beginning here, we think ahead to the actual paper we will be writing. The first paragraph of a short paper should include the thesis and any general statements related to it.

As we read over our list, we see that the statements express ideas about two kinds of living arrangements—on-campus living and off-campus living. One of the statements, more general than the others, deals with both kinds. It is number _____. □

6

For now, mark statement 6 with a check. Of the remaining nine statements, some have to do with on-campus living, others have to do with off-campus living. Notice that most of these statements have to do with (on-campus, off-campus) living. □

off-campus

The reason for there being more statements about off-campus living lies in the thesis. Read it again carefully. The conclusion it aims at is not that on-campus living is expensive but that off-campus living can be (more, less) expensive. □

less

When organizing our outline, we must keep our thesis—and the conclusion it aims at—firmly in mind. It is logical that, since the conclusion will come last, the statements about (on-campus, off-campus) living will come last. □

off-campus

The statements about on-campus living, then, will come first. Refer to the list. There are three of them: numbers _____, _____, and _____. □

1, 3, 5

For convenience, mark all these statements with a capital A on the list. Here they are:

A _____ *Students living on campus may pay twice as much for room and board as they need to.*

A _____ *Incidental expenses for such necessities as laundry and extra meals can add as much as $500 to the cost of dorm living.*

A _____ *Room and board at a dorm costs $1,000 for the two semesters.*

These statements will be the basis for the second paragraph of the paper we will write. However, we need to arrange them so that the most general statement comes first and the others logically follow. Find the most general statement and mark it number 1. Of the two remaining statements, one logically comes before the other. Mark it number 2. Then mark the remaining statement number 3. ☐

1, 3, 2 (The third statement logically comes before the second because it contains the major cost.)

The remaining six statements are all about off-campus living. But in reading them over, we see that they are about two kinds of living arrangements—living in _____ and living at _____. ☐

an apartment
home

Logically, the statements about the two kinds of living arrangements need to be in separate paragraphs. Our question now is, which should come before the other, the paragraph with the statements about living in an apartment or those about living at home? Here, we don't have to look very far to find a logical order. Since we began with a paragraph about the most expensive living arrangement—on-campus living—the next paragraph should be about the next most expensive living arrangement, living (in an apartment, at home). ☐

in an apartment

Mark all the statements about living in an apartment with a capital B. There are three of them: numbers ____, ____, and ____. ☐

4, 8, 10

    B ____ *Apartments, though expensive, can be shared comfortably by a group of students for as little as $35 a month rent.*

    B ____ *A student living in an apartment can buy enough food for himself for less than $25 a month, if he is careful when shopping.*

    B ____ *A careful student can live for less than $80 a month in a shared apartment.*

Here are the statements marked B. Notice that it is fairly easy to organize them in a logical sequence beginning with the one containing the total cost figure—the most general statement—and then arranging the other two according to the amounts they contain. Number them accordingly. ☐

2, 3, 1

Here are the remaining three statements, those about living at home. Mark them with a capital C on the list.

    C ____ *Living at home while going to school is usually the most economical arrangement for a student.*

    C ____ *When living at home, students whose parents can afford it often do not pay room and board.*

    C ____ *If his family lets a student live at home, even his incidental expenses will be lower.*

Once again we have a general statement and two particular statements that have a logical order. Number the sequence accordingly. ☐

1, 2, 3

Here is our complete outline:

Thesis: *Living off campus can be much more economical than living on campus in a dormitory.*

Room and board costs make the difference in the cost of education because the rest of the charges for education are the same for students living on or off campus.

A1. *Students living on campus may pay twice as much for room and board as they need to.*

A2. *Room and board at a dorm costs $1,000 for the two semesters.*

A3. *Incidental expenses for such necessities as laundry and extra meals can add as much as $500 to the cost of dorm living.*

B1. *A careful student can live for less than $80 a month in a shared apartment.*

B2. *Apartments, though expensive, can be shared comfortably by a group of students for as little as $35 a month rent.*

B3. *A student living in an apartment can buy enough food for himself for less than $25 a month, if he is careful when shopping.*

C1. *Living at home while going to school is usually the most economical arrangement for a student.*

C2. *When living at home, students whose parents can afford it often do not pay room and board.*

C3. *If his family lets a student live at home, even his incidental expenses will be lower.*

Here we have a working outline. As crude as it is, you can see in it the shape of the final essay, much of it already written. Of course, some sentences will have to be combined and rewritten, and other sentences will have to be added. We'll be taking up such matters in the next section. □

No response is needed.

WRITING THE ESSAY

In this section we are going to write a short essay, beginning with the very first step—finding a subject—and continuing through all the steps until we have finished the job. Since we'll be going over all the kinds of choices dealt with in this text, you'll be able to see how each choice, wisely made, leads to the ultimate goal of a well-written essay.

Suppose you were given this list of general subjects:

1. *The manufacture of inks*
2. *Local civil rights disputes*
3. *New theories in astrology*
4. *Education of retarded children*
5. *Pollution of natural resources*

2, 5 Probably only two of these subjects are suitable for a non-specialist to tackle, numbers _____ and _____ . □

Let's assume that you chose number 5 as your general subject: *Pollution of natural resources.* Obviously, as it stands, the

broad subject is too (broad, narrow) for a short essay. □

1. *Pollution of the air*
2. *Pollution of Lake Monarch*
3. *Pollution of rivers near large cities*
4. *Pollution of beaches on the southern coasts*

2 Only one of these items is limited enough for a short essay, number _____ . □

In *Pollution of Lake Monarch*, we have a subject limited enough for a short essay. Now we need to decide what we are going to say about the subject. Our next step, then, is to write a general statement which includes our subject and an expression of our purpose in writing the essay. This statement will be our

thesis _____ . □

The pollution of Lake Monarch is an extremely serious problem with interesting causes.

As a thesis, this statement is almost useless because it is too (general, particular). ☐

The pollution of Lake Monarch is serious because fishermen can no longer catch edible fish there.

This statement is also useless because it deals with only a limited effect of the pollution and is therefore too (general, particular). ☐

Migrating ducks no longer pause at Lake Monarch because it has become so badly polluted.
Polluted by tons of raw sewage, Lake Monarch is rapidly becoming a foul-smelling cesspool.
Chemical changes have made a substantial difference in the quality of the water in Lake Monarch.

Only one of these statements is a satisfactory thesis, the (first, second, third). ☐

Now that we have a thesis, we can begin snowballing until we have a list of a dozen or more statements that fit the thesis. Keep the thesis firmly in mind as you choose statements for the list.

Thesis: *Polluted by tons of raw sewage, Lake Monarch is rapidly becoming a foul-smelling cesspool.*

Most of the sewage flows into Lake Monarch from the Blue River.
Federal guidelines for flood control planning vary from region to region.

Only one of these statements should be on our list, the (first, second). ☐

In Lake Monarch the proliferation of algae has strangled all but a few hardy survivors of the fish that once abounded.
Nearby Lake Mohawk has a severe problem with the growth of algae also.

Only one of these statements should be on our list, the (first, second). ☐

At this stage of the writing process, don't worry about the phrasing. You can correct that later if necessary, while you do the actual writing.

> *Pilots flying over the region can easily spot Lake Monarch because of its unusual shape.*
>
> *Lake Monarch is on its last legs.*

Only one of these statements should be on our list, the (first, **second**). ☐

> *Maggots, mosquitoes, and bloodworms multiply in the poisonous soup near shore.*
>
> *Bacteria such as* Salmonella *multiply near the shore also.*

(The first, The second, **Both**, Neither) statement(s) should be on our list. ☐

> *The original explorers in the region used Lake Monarch as a headquarters for exploration farther west.*
>
> *Lake Monarch can be saved and restored to health only if the cities upstream are forced by law to stop using the Blue River as a convenient sewer for their growing populations.*

(The first, **The second**, Both, Neither) statement(s) should be on our list. ☐

> *Deer-hunting season in the Lake Monarch area lasts for six weeks in the fall.*
>
> *Along the shoreline, the once sandy beaches are becoming places of mud and sewage.*

(The first, **The second**, Both, Neither) statement(s) should be on our list. ☐

> *The operators of the two large resorts on Lake Monarch*
> *Very few trout have ever been caught in Lake Monarch.*

(The first, The second, Both, **Neither**) item(s) should be on our list. ☐

There are several important rivers in the Lake Monarch region.
The population of Crescent City has grown from 10,000 thirty
years ago to the present 150,000, and its sewage, which flows
into Lake Monarch from the Blue River, has increased with its
rising population.

(The first, The second, Both, Neither) statement(s) should be on
our list. ☐   *The second*

In sewage, the chemicals that do the most damage to a lake
are phosphorus from household detergents and nitrogen.
Large quantities of phosphorus and nitrogen mean the rapid
growth of algae.

(The first, The second, Both, Neither) statement(s) should be on
our list. ☐   *Both*

Five small towns farther upstream from Crescent City pump
into the Blue River twenty million gallons of untreated sewage
a day.
In the Lake Monarch area, dairy farming is one of the primary
occupations.

(The first, The second, Both, Neither) statement(s) should be on
our list. ☐   *The first*

When algae die, they sink to the bottom and decay, using up
the oxygen in the deep water necessary for the survival of fish.
Lake Monarch will be dead in ten years if the dumping of
sewage continues even at the present rate.

(The first, The second, Both, Neither) statement(s) should be on
our list. ☐   *Both*

Walleye, bass, perch, and whitefish
Most of the sewage flowing into the lake settles there.

(The first, The second, Both, Neither) item(s) should be on our
list. ☐   *The second*

Here is our completed list:

Thesis: *Polluted by tons of raw sewage, Lake Monarch is rapidly becoming a foul-smelling cesspool.*

1. *Most of the sewage flows into Lake Monarch from the Blue River.*
2. *In Lake Monarch the proliferation of algae has strangled all but a few hardy survivors of the fish that once abounded.*
3. *Lake Monarch is on its last legs.*
4. *Maggots, mosquitoes, and bloodworms multiply in the poisonous soup near shore.*
5. *Bacteria such as* Salmonella *multiply near the shore also.*
6. *Lake Monarch can be saved and restored to health only if the cities upstream are forced by law to stop using the Blue River as a convenient sewer for their growing populations.*
7. *Along the shoreline, the once sandy beaches are becoming places of mud and sewage.*
8. *The population of Crescent City has grown from 10,000 thirty years ago to the present 150,000, and its sewage, which flows into Lake Monarch from the Blue River, has increased with its rising population.*
9. *In sewage, the chemicals that do the most damage to a lake are phosphorus from household detergents and nitrogen.*
10. *Large quantities of phosphorus and nitrogen mean the rapid growth of algae.*
11. *Five small towns farther upstream from Crescent City pump into the Blue River twenty million gallons of untreated sewage a day.*
12. *When algae die, they sink to the bottom and decay, using up the oxygen in the deep water necessary for the survival of fish.*

13. *Lake Monarch will be dead in ten years if the dumping of sewage continues even at the present rate.*

14. *Most of the sewage flowing into the lake settles there.*

Our next step is to (begin writing, make a rough outline). ☐

make a rough outline

To make a rough outline, we first identify the most general statement or statements on our list that are related to the thesis. We have one such statement, number _____. ☐

3

Statement 3 will be the first on our outline. For now, mark it with a check. Most of the remaining statements have to do with the present condition of the lake. However, two of them have to do with its future, numbers _____ and _____. ☐

6, 13

Statements about the future condition of the lake are conclusions based on the statements about its present condition. Therefore, they should logically be placed (first, last) in the essay. ☐

last

For now, mark statements 6 and 13 with an X to identify them. Now look at the remaining eleven statements. Some have to do with the effect of sewage on the water—the growth of algae—others with the effect on or near the shore, and others with the source of the sewage. Which of the three groups should logically come first?

_____

_____ ☐

the group having to do with the source of the sewage

Four statements provide information about where the sewage comes from and where it settles: numbers _____, _____, _____, and _____. ☐

1, 8, 11, 14

Mark these statements with a capital A. Here they are:

A_____ *The population of Crescent City has grown from 10,000 thirty years ago to the present 150,000, and its sewage, which flows into Lake Monarch from the Blue River, has increased with its rising population.*

A_____ *Most of the sewage flows into Lake Monarch from the Blue River.*

A_____ *Most of the sewage flowing into the lake settles there.*

A_____ *Five small towns farther upstream from Crescent City pump into the Blue River twenty million gallons of untreated sewage a day.*

Mark the most general statement about the source of the sewage number 1. Of the three remaining statements, two have to do with the source of the sewage from particular places. Number them 2 and 3 logically. Then number the remaining statement 4. ☐

2, 1, 4, 3

Two groups of statements remain. One is about the effect of the sewage on the lake water, the other about its effect on or near shore. In reading them over, particularly statement 9, which group seems more important and logically first?

the statements about the effect

of sewage on the water _____

_____ ☐

Four statements are about the effect of sewage on water (the growth and decay of algae), numbers _____, _____, _____, and _____. ☐

2, 9, 10, 12

Mark these four statements with a capital B on the list. Here they are:

B _____ *In Lake Monarch the proliferation of algae has strangled all but a few hardy survivors of the fish that once abounded.*

B _____ *In sewage, the chemicals that do the most damage to a lake are phosphorus from household detergents and nitrogen.*

B _____ *Large quantities of phosphorus and nitrogen mean the rapid growth of algae.*

B _____ *When algae die, they sink to the bottom and decay, using up the oxygen in the deep water necessary for the survival of fish.*

Of these four statements, one is more general because it tells why sewage is particularly damaging. Mark this statement number 1. The remaining three statements have a logical sequence, connecting the chemicals to the growth and decay of algae and finally the effect of that decay on a particular lake. Number these remaining statements accordingly. ☐

4, 1, 2, 3

Three statements remain. Mark them with a capital C on the list. Here they are:

C _____ *Maggots, mosquitoes, and bloodworms multiply in the poisonous soup near shore.*

C _____ *Bacteria such as* Salmonella *multiply near the shore also.*

C _____ *Along the shoreline, the once sandy beaches are becoming places of mud and sewage.*

One of these three statements is more general than the others because it describes generally the effect of pollution around the shore. Mark this statement number 1. The remaining two statements have a logical order because of the word *also* in the last. Number them accordingly. ☐

2, 3, 1

All we need to do now is look again at the statements we marked X in the beginning. Mark these now with a capital D. Here they are:

D _____ *Lake Monarch can be saved and restored to health only if the cities upstream are forced by law to stop using the Blue River as a convenient sewer for their growing populations.*

D _____ *Lake Monarch will be dead in ten years if the dumping of sewage continues even at the present rate.*

Both these statements are just about equally general, but there is a logical sequence for them to follow. Number them accordingly. □

2, 1

We have now completed our rough working outline. Here it is:

Thesis: *Polluted by tons of raw sewage, Lake Monarch is rapidly becoming a foul-smelling cesspool.*

Lake Monarch is on its last legs.

A1. *Most of the sewage flows into Lake Monarch from the Blue River.*

A2. *The population of Crescent City has grown from 10,000 thirty years ago to the present 150,000, and its sewage, which flows into Lake Monarch from the Blue River, has increased with its rising population.*

A3. *Five small towns farther upstream from Crescent City pump into the Blue River twenty million gallons of untreated sewage a day.*

A4. *Most of the sewage flowing into the lake settles there.*

B1. *In sewage, the chemicals that do the most damage to a lake are phosphorus from household detergents and nitrogen.*

B2. *Large quantities of phosphorus and nitrogen mean the rapid growth of algae.*

B3. *When algae die, they sink to the bottom and decay, using up the oxygen in the deep water necessary for the survival of fish.*

B4. *In Lake Monarch the proliferation of algae has strangled all but a few hardy survivors of the fish that once abounded.*

C1. *Along the shoreline, the once sandy beaches are becoming places of mud and sewage.*

C2. *Maggots, mosquitoes, and bloodworms multiply in the poisonous soup near shore.*

C3. *Bacteria such as* Salmonella *multiply near the shore also.*

D1. *Lake Monarch will be dead in ten years if the dumping of sewage continues even at the present rate.*

D2. *Lake Monarch can be saved and restored to health only if the cities upstream are forced by law to stop using the Blue River as a convenient sewer for their growing populations.* □

No response is required.

Having prepared our outline, we are ready to begin writing. And we begin with the thesis and its related sentence, which form the skeleton of our introductory paragraph.

Polluted by tons of raw sewage, Lake Monarch is rapidly becoming a foul-smelling cesspool.

Lake Monarch is on its last legs.

One of the sentences should be the topic sentence of our introductory paragraph because it is more general than the other, the (first, second). □

second

Lake Monarch is on its last legs.

This statement is general enough to be a topic sentence, but as it stands it's probably one of the worst sentences ever written. Lakes don't have legs. The problem is that *on its last legs* is (too abstract, a cliché). □

a cliché

Let's look for a good replacement for *on its last legs.* Here are two possibilities, both having more or less the same meaning:

Lake Monarch is (dying, moribund).

moribund
dying

One of these choices is a lot fancier than the other, (*dying, moribund*). The preferable choice, then, is (*dying, moribund*). ☐

Lake Monarch is dying.

This statement, its language simple and direct, is a satisfactory topic sentence for our introductory paragraph. The topic is

Lake Monarch   dying

_____ and the key is _____. ☐

We could now add the thesis to this topic sentence and have an introductory paragraph of sorts, but it would lack enough general information to help the reader identify the lake and the extent of its change.

condition of nearby lakes
location of the lake
former condition of the lake

Information of two of these three kinds would be useful in the introductory paragraph, the (first and second, second and

second and third

third). ☐

Lake Monarch is dying. **Until recently Lake Monarch was pure and inviting.**

adds information about part of
the sentence before

For now, ignore the awkward repetition of *Lake Monarch.* We can add this sentence because it (follows topic and key, adds information about part of the sentence before). ☐

Lake Monarch is dying. Until recently Lake Monarch was pure and inviting. **It was enjoyed by swimmers and fishermen from the time of the first settlers.**

adds information about part of
the sentence before

We can add this sentence because it (follows topic and key, adds information about part of the sentence before). ☐

> *Lake Monarch is dying. Until recently Lake Monarch was*
> *pure and inviting. It was enjoyed by swimmers and fishermen*
> *from the time of the first settlers.*

Before continuing, let's look at a possibility we've ignored. We can combine the two sentences we've added in two different ways. We can, for instance, make the second sentence into a verb cluster based on the *-ed* verb already there and attach it to the first sentence:

> *Until recently Lake Monarch was pure and inviting,*

_____

_____

_____. ☐

enjoyed by swimmers and

fishermen from the time

of the first settlers

> *Until recently Lake Monarch was pure and inviting.*
> *It was enjoyed by swimmers and fishermen from the time*
> *of the first settlers.*

Our other alternative is to take the adjective cluster from the first sentence and embed it into the second by attaching it to the beginning:

> *Until recently* _____, *it was enjoyed*
> *by swimmers and fishermen from the time of the first*
> *settlers.* ☐

pure and inviting

> *Until recently Lake Monarch was pure and inviting, enjoyed*
> *by swimmers and fishermen from the time of the first*
> *settlers.*
> *Until recently pure and inviting, it was enjoyed by swimmers*
> *and fishermen from the time of the first settlers.*

In the first sentence the focus is on the lake's being (pure and inviting, enjoyed). In the second it is on its being (pure and inviting, enjoyed). ☐

pure and inviting

enjoyed

Until recently Lake Monarch was pure and inviting, enjoyed by swimmers and fishermen from the time of the first settlers. Until recently pure and inviting, it was enjoyed by swimmers and fishermen from the time of the first settlers.

The key of our paragraph—*dying*—guides us in our choice of focus. Since the key has to do with the condition of the lake, the better choice for the focus is the lake's being (pure and inviting, enjoyed). □

pure and inviting

Lake Monarch is dying. Until recently Lake Monarch was pure and inviting, enjoyed by swimmers and fishermen from the time of the first settlers.

To get rid of the awkward repetition of *Lake Monarch*, we can find a synonym to use in the second sentence:

Until recently (this large body of water, this large lake) was pure and inviting. . . .

One of these choices links the first and second sentence more closely together, (*this large body of water, this large lake*). □

this large lake

*Lake Monarch is dying. Until recently this large lake was pure and inviting, enjoyed by swimmers and fishermen from the time of the first settlers. **It is in the northwest corner of the state.***

We can add this sentence to the paragraph because it (follows topic and key, adds information about part of the sentence before). □

adds information about part of the sentence before

Lake Monarch is dying. Until recently this large lake was pure and inviting, enjoyed by swimmers and fishermen from the time of the first settlers. **It is in the northwest corner of the state.**

We can add this sentence as it is, but the result is a clumsy sequence since the last sentence carries only incidental information. Before we add such sentences, we should look around for a way to embed the important part from them into previous sentences, and here we can do the job quite easily:

Until recently this large lake _____

_____ *was pure and inviting, . . .* ☐

in the northwest corner of the state

Lake Monarch is dying. Until recently this large lake in the northwest corner of the state was pure and inviting, enjoyed by swimmers and fishermen from the time of the first settlers. **Polluted by tons of raw sewage, it is rapidly becoming a foul-smelling cesspool.**

Here we've added the thesis. We can add it to the paragraph because it (follows topic and key, adds information about part of the sentence before). ☐

follows topic and key

Lake Monarch is dying. Until recently this large lake in the northwest corner of the state was pure and inviting, enjoyed by swimmers and fishermen from the time of the first settlers. **Polluted by tons of raw sewage, it is rapidly becoming a foul-smelling cesspool.**

Adding the thesis here causes a slight problem because the sentence before it carries information about a former condition. To connect these two sentences smoothly, we can use a linker, and the best choice would be (*Therefore, Now*). ☐

Now

Lake Monarch is dying . . . . Now, polluted by tons of raw sewage, it is rapidly becoming a foul-smelling cesspool. **Wildlife sickens there. Swimmers and fishermen venture there at their risk.**

Here we've added two sentences. They fit the paragraph because they (follow topic and key, add information about part of the sentence before). ☐

follow topic and key

> *Lake Monarch is dying. . . . Now, polluted by tons of raw*
> *sewage, it is rapidly becoming a foul-smelling cesspool.*
> **Wildlife sickens there. Swimmers and fishermen venture**
> **there at their risk.**

Though both added sentences follow topic and key, the information they contain is incidental. To maintain focus, we can make both into adverb clauses joined to the sentence before:

> *Now, polluted by tons of raw sewage, it is rapidly becoming*
> *a foul-smelling cesspool where* _____

wildlife sickens

> *and where* _____

swimmers and fishermen venture

at their risk

> _____ . ☐

Our introductory paragraph is complete. It contains the thesis as well as enough information about the lake's past and present condition so that the reader knows the general problem before he begins the second paragraph.

> *Lake Monarch is dying. Until recently this large lake in the*
> *northwest corner of the state was pure and inviting, enjoyed*
> *by swimmers and fishermen from the time of the first settlers.*
> *Now, polluted by tons of raw sewage, it is rapidly becoming a*
> *foul-smelling cesspool, where wildlife sickens and where*

No response is needed.

> *swimmers and fishermen venture at their risk.* ☐

Now let's return to our outline. The group of sentences we've marked A will become our second paragraph. Statement A1 will be our topic sentence.

> *Most of the sewage flows into Lake Monarch from the*
> *Blue River.*

of the sewage

The topic is *Most* _____ .

into Lake Monarch from the

The key is *(flows)* _____

Blue River

_____ . ☐

Sentence A2, however, presents problems.

The population of Crescent City has grown from 10,000 thirty years ago to the present 150,000, and its sewage, which flows into Lake Monarch from the Blue River, has increased with its rising population.

The sentence begins with information about Crescent City's population, which (does, does not) immediately connect to the topic sentence. ☐ | *does not*

What we need is a sentence connecting Crescent City to the problem of sewage in the Blue River, our topic and key.

Most of the raw sewage flows into Lake Monarch from the Blue River.

Crescent City has a sewage plant that is capable of treating only half of the sewage it processes.

The biggest source of the sewage is Crescent City.

Only one of these sentences follows topic and key, the (first, second). ☐ | *second*

Most of the sewage flows into Lake Monarch from the Blue River. The biggest source of the sewage is Crescent City. **It is five miles upstream from the lake.**

Here we have added still another sentence. We can because it (follows topic and key, adds information about part of the sentence before). ☐ | *adds information about part of the sentence before*

The biggest source of the sewage is Crescent City. **It is five miles upstream from the lake.**

The added sentence here provides only incidental information and, as usual, we should look for a way to combine it with the sentence before. And it's easily done. We can take the information from the added sentence and embed it into the sentence before simply by attaching it to the end:

The biggest source of the sewage is Crescent City,

_____. ☐ | *five miles upstream from the lake*

Now we can add sentence A2. But there is part of the sentence we don't need because of the sentence we've just written.

> *The biggest source of the sewage is Crescent City, five miles upstream from the lake.* **The population of Crescent City has grown from 10,000 thirty years ago to the present 150,000, and its sewage, which flows into Lake Monarch from the Blue River, has increased with its rising population.**

which flows into Lake Monarch from the Blue River

Identify the part of the added sentence we don't need. ☐

sewage

Return to the outline. Notice that sentence A3 has some particular information about the five smaller towns that is lacking in sentence A2 about Crescent City, the amount of _____. ☐

It will be helpful to add here a sentence about the amount of sewage coming from Crescent City.

> *Now Crescent City pumps partly treated sewage into the Blue River at the rate of fifty million gallons a day.*
> *The amount of sewage produced by Crescent City in a day is fifty million gallons.*

first

One of these sentences will serve our purpose better because it follows topic and key, the (first, second). ☐

> *The population of Crescent City has grown from 10,000 thirty years ago to the present 150,000, and its sewage, which flows into Lake Monarch from the Blue River, has increased with its rising population.* **Now Crescent City pumps partly treated sewage into the Blue River at the rate of fifty million gallons a day.**

We've repeated *Crescent City* in connected sentences, so it would be wise to replace it with another phrase, one that will link the added sentence to the one before.

> *Now (the city, this metropolis) pumps partly treated sewage into the Blue River at the rate of fifty million gallons a day.*

the city

The better choice is *(the city, this metropolis)*. ☐

Now we can add sentence A3.

> *Most of the sewage flows into Lake Monarch from the Blue River. . . . Now the city pumps partly treated sewage into the Blue River at the rate of fifty million gallons a day.* **Five small towns farther upstream from Crescent City pump into the Blue River twenty million gallons of untreated sewage a day.**

Since we've already mentioned Crescent City, a phrase in this sentence is unnecessary. Identify it. ☐ | *from Crescent City*

> *Most of the sewage flows into Lake Monarch from the Blue River. . . . Now the city pumps partly treated sewage into the Blue River at the rate of fifty million gallons a day.* **(In addition, Thus), five small towns farther upstream pump into the Blue River twenty million gallons of untreated sewage a day.**

The last two sentences would fit together more smoothly with a linker signaling their connection. Since the last sentence expresses a (similar, contrasting) idea, the better linker is *(In addition, Thus).* ☐ | *similar* / *In addition*

Now we can add our final sentence, *Most of the sewage flowing into the lake settles there.* But as it stands, the sentence (does, does not) give the reader a clear picture of the accumulation. ☐ | *does not*

> *Most of the sewage flows into Lake Monarch from the Blue River. . . . Most of the sewage flowing into the lake settles there.* **Each day's flood adds another wave of crap to the water and beaches.**

Ignore the phrasing for a moment. We can add this sentence because it (follows topic and key, adds information about part of the sentence before). ☐ | *adds information about part of the sentence before*

> *Each day's flood adds another wave of crap to the water and beaches.*

The one word that stands out here is _____, a word that's not useful in this essay because it is (a cliché, slang). ☐ | *crap* / *slang*

Each day's flood adds another wave of (stuff, waste and poisons).

waste and poisons
concrete

The better replacement for this sentence is *(stuff, waste and poisons)* because it is more (concrete, abstract). ☐

Most of the sewage flows into Lake Monarch from the Blue River. . . . **Most of the sewage flowing into the lake settles there. Each day's flood adds another wave of waste and poisons to the water and beaches.**

Since we have now a sentence adding incidental information, we should look for a way to embed it into the one before. We can do it by making the **added** sentence into an absolute phrase based on an *-ing* verb:

Most of the sewage flowing into the lake settles there, each

*day's flood adding another wave
of waste and poisons to the
water and beaches*

_____

_____

_____. ☐

We've now completed our second paragraph. Let's look it over before going on.

Most of the sewage flows into Lake Monarch from the Blue River. The biggest source of the sewage is Crescent City, five miles upstream from the lake. The population of Crescent City has grown from 10,000 thirty years ago to the present 150,000, and its sewage has increased with the rising population. Now the city pumps partly treated sewage into the Blue River at the rate of fifty million gallons a day. In addition, five small towns farther upstream pump into the Blue River twenty million gallons of untreated sewage a day. Most of the sewage flowing into the lake settles there, each day's flood adding another wave of waste and poisons to the water and beaches. ☐

No response is needed.

Once again, return to the outline. Our next paragraph will be based on the statements marked B. The first of these, the most general, will be the topic sentence:

In sewage, the chemicals that do the most damage to a lake are phosphorus from household detergents and nitrogen.

The topic is *the*_____

_____ | *chemicals that do the most damage to a lake*

The key is_____

_____. □ | *phosphorus from household detergents and nitrogen*

In sewage, the chemicals that do the most damage to a lake are phosphorus from household detergents and nitrogen.
Large quantities of phosphorus and nitrogen mean the rapid growth of algae.
Here we've added statement B2. We can add it because it (follows topic and key, adds information about part of the sentence before). □ | *adds information about part of the sentence before*

In sewage, the chemicals that do the most damage to a lake are phosphorus from household detergents and nitrogen.
Large quantities of phosphorus and nitrogen mean the rapid growth of algae.
Repeating *phosphorus and nitrogen* in these sentences is unnecessary and awkward.

Large quantities of these (chemicals, elements) mean the rapid growth of algae.

The choice of a substitution that will link these sentences more closely together is *(chemicals, elements)*. □ | *chemicals*

Large quantities of these chemicals mean the rapid growth of algae.

Another problem with this sentence is that it contains a scientific term needing some explanation for a general audience, _____. □ | *algae*

When we find it necessary to use an unfamiliar scientific term, we should explain it.

Some algae are poisonous, and contact with them should be avoided.

Algae are an extremely small form of plant life.

Only one of these sentences will serve our purpose of explaining the term *algae*, the (first, second). ☐

second

Large quantities of these chemicals mean the rapid growth of algae. **Algae are an extremely small form of plant life.**

Since the added sentence gives only incidental information, we should embed it into the sentence it follows. Here we can make the added sentence into a noun cluster and add it to the other, more important sentence:

Large quantities of these chemicals mean the rapid growth of algae, _____

an extremely small form of
plant life

_____. ☐

Large quantities of these chemicals mean the rapid growth of algae, an extremely small form of plant life. **The presence of algae turns healthy clear lake water into a muddy green.**

We can add the new sentence here because it (follows topic and key, adds information about part of the sentence before). ☐

adds information about part of
the sentence before

Large quantities of these chemicals mean the rapid growth of algae, an extremely small form of plant life. **The presence of algae turns healthy clear lake water into a muddy green.**

Once again we have a sentence with incidental information. We can embed it into the one before by changing part of it into a relative clause:

Large quantities of these chemicals mean the rapid growth of algae, an extremely small form of plant life that _____

turns healthy clear lake water
into a muddy green

_____. ☐

In sewage, the chemicals that do the most damage to a lake are phosphorus from household detergents and nitrogen. . . . **When algae die, they sink to the bottom and decay, using up the oxygen in the deep water necessary for the survival of fish.** Here we've added statement B3 from our outline. We can add it because it (follows topic and key, adds information about part of the sentence before). ☐

follows topic and key

In sewage, the chemicals that do the most damage to a lake are phosphorus from household detergents and nitrogen. . . . **In Lake Monarch the proliferation of algae has strangled all but a few hardy survivors of the fish that once abounded.** Here we've added statement B4 from our outline. We can add it because it (follows topic and key, adds information about part of the sentence before). ☐

follows topic and key

In Lake Monarch the proliferation of algae has strangled all but a few hardy survivors of the fish that once abounded. One problem with this sentence as it stands is that it contains a rather fancy word, _____. ☐

proliferation

We could substitute *growth* for *proliferation*, but the fancier word connotes more than the simpler one. *Proliferation* refers especially to wild, uncontrolled growth. We have to choose, then, between a somewhat fancy word that suits our meaning perfectly and a simpler word that doesn't quite do the job. Which do you choose? _____ ☐

Either choice is satisfactory.
We'll assume, however, that
proliferation won't cause
readers too much trouble.

In Lake Monarch the proliferation of algae has strangled all but a few hardy survivors of the fish that once abounded. Another word in this sentence, though not wrong in any way, is fairly abstract, _____. ☐

fish

Since we're talking about fish in a particular lake, it would be wise to give our readers some concrete idea of what fish are dying there.

In Lake Monarch the proliferation of algae has strangled all but a few hardy survivors of (the various kinds of fish that live there, the walleye, bass, perch, and whitefish) that once abounded.

the walleye, bass, perch, and whitefish

Of the two choices, the more concrete is *(the various kinds of fish that live there, the walleye, bass, perch, and whitefish).* ☐

Here, then, is our third paragraph, complete.

In sewage, the chemicals that do the most damage to a lake are phosphorus from household detergents and nitrogen. Large quantities of these chemicals mean the rapid growth of algae, an extremely small form of plant life that turns healthy clear lake water into a muddy green. When algae die, they sink to the bottom and decay, using up the oxygen in the deep water necessary for the survival of fish. In Lake Monarch the proliferation of algae has strangled all but a few hardy survivors of the walleye, bass, perch, and whitefish that once abounded. ☐

No response is required.

Turn once more to the outline. Our next paragraph will be based on the statements marked C.

Along the shoreline, the once sandy beaches are becoming places of mud and sewage.

Here is statement C1, which will be our topic sentence. The

the once sandy beaches

topic is _____ .

places of mud and sewage

The key is _____ . ☐

Along the shoreline, the once sandy beaches are becoming places of mud and sewage.

Though a good topic sentence, this statement has one word too

places

abstract for our purpose, _____ . ☐

Along the shoreline, the once sandy beaches are becoming (repositories, quagmires) of mud and sewage.

Both the alternate choices, *repositories* and *quagmires*, are more (abstract, concrete) than *places*. ☐ — *concrete*

Of the two alternatives, *repositories* has a(n) (pleasant, unpleasant) connotation, and *quagmires* has a(n) (pleasant, unpleasant) connotation. ☐ — *pleasant*

unpleasant

Think for a minute. In describing the shoreline here, do we want a word with a pleasant connotation or one with an unpleasant connotation? The better choice for the sentence, then, is *(quagmires, repositories)*. ☐ — *quagmires*

Along the shoreline, the once sandy beaches are becoming quagmires of mud and sewage. **Pools of chemicals collect there.**

Though not on our outline, we can add this sentence to the paragraph because it (follows topic and key, adds information about part of the sentence before). ☐ — *follows topic and key*

Pools of chemicals collect there.

One word in this sentence is fairly abstract, _____. ☐ — *chemicals*

Among water-polluting chemicals are calcium, sodium, sulfur, mercury, potassium, phenols, aldehydes, sulfates, chlorides, chromates, fluorides, and acids of various kinds as well as the more complex chemicals of pesticides and weed killers. You get the idea. In a short essay such as we are writing, concrete mention of each polluting chemical (is, is not) necessary. ☐ — *is not*

Along the shoreline, the once sandy beaches are becoming quagmires of mud and sewage. Pools of chemicals collect there. **These chemicals add powerfully to the stench of rotting organic waste.**

Again, though not on our outline, we can add this sentence because it (follows topic and key, adds information about part of the sentence before). ☐ — *adds information about part of the sentence before*

Pools of chemicals collect there. **These chemicals add powerfully to the stench of rotting organic waste.**

Here once again we have an added sentence that gives incidental information. We can embed it into the sentence it follows by making it into a verb cluster based on the *-ing* form of its verb:

Pools of chemicals collect there, _____

_____. □

adding powerfully to the stench of rotting organic waste

Along the shoreline, the once sandy beaches are becoming quagmires of mud and sewage. Pools of chemicals collect there, adding powerfully to the stench of rotting organic waste. **Soggy paper, rusted cans, and broken milk cartons lie half-buried in the mud.**

We can add this sentence, not on our outline, because it (follows topic and key, adds information about part of the sentence before). □

follows topic and key

Along the shoreline, the once sandy beaches are becoming quagmires of mud and sewage. . . . **Maggots, mosquitoes, and bloodworms multiply in the poisonous soup near shore.**

Here we've added statement C2 from our outline. We can add it because it (follows topic and key, adds information about part of the sentence before). □

follows topic and key

Along the shoreline, the once sandy beaches are becoming quagmires of mud and sewage. . . . Maggots, mosquitoes, and bloodworms multiply in the poisonous soup near shore. **Bacteria such as Salmonella multiply near the shore also.**

Now we've added statement C3 from our outline. We can add it because it (follows topic and key, adds information about part of the sentence before). □

follows topic and key

Maggots, mosquitoes, and bloodworms multiply in the poisonous soup near shore. Bacteria such as Salmonella *multiply near the shore also.*

These two sentences make an awkward sequence because key words are repeated. To avoid this awkwardness, we can combine them into one sentence, embedding the information from the second into the first:

Maggots, mosquitoes, and bloodworms multiply in the poisonous soup near shore, as well as _____

_____. ☐   *bacteria such as Salmonella*

Maggots, mosquitoes, and bloodworms multiply in the poisonous soup near shore, as well as bacteria such as Salmonella.

Only one of the words in this sentence would be unfamiliar to non-scientists, _____. ☐   *Salmonella*

We could go into the more complex effects of bacteria *Salmonella*, but in a short essay a brief statement of its general dangers is enough.

Maggots, mosquitoes, and bloodworms multiply in the poisonous soup near shore, as well as bacteria such as Salmonella. **Bacteria such as Salmonella make the water unsafe even for swimming.**

We can add this sentence because it (follows topic and key, adds information about part of the sentence before). ☐   *adds information about part of the sentence before*

*Maggots, mosquitoes, and bloodworms multiply in the
poisonous soup near shore, as well as bacteria such as
Salmonella.* **Bacteria such as Salmonella make the water
unsafe even for swimming.**

Adding this sentence involves some awkward repetition we can
avoid by making it into a relative clause and embedding it into
the first sentence:

*Maggots, mosquitoes, and bloodworms multiply in the
poisonous soup near shore, as well as bacteria such as*
Salmonella, *which* _____

_____. □

*make the water unsafe even for
swimming*

Here is our fourth paragraph:

*Along the shoreline, the once sandy beaches are becoming
quagmires of mud and sewage. Pools of chemicals collect
there, adding powerfully to the stench of rotting organic
waste. Soggy paper, rusted cans, and broken milk cartons
lie half-buried in the mud. Maggots, mosquitoes, and bloodworms multiply in the poisonous soup near shore, as well as
bacteria such as* Salmonella, *which make the water unsafe
even for swimming.* □

No response is required.

Now we can turn to our outline and write the final paragraph,
which will be based on the two statements marked D. Statement
D1 will be our topic sentence:

*Lake Monarch will be dead in ten years if the dumping of
sewage continues even at its present rate.*

This sentence has a long adverb clause that we can move to
another position. It begins with the word _____ and runs to the
end. □

if

Lake Monarch will be dead in ten years if the dumping of
sewage continues even at its present rate.

Remember, placing movable parts in a position other than normal emphasizes the entire sentence. Since this sentence is one of the most important in the essay, we should emphasize it. Rearrange its parts for emphasis:

_____

_____

_____

_____ ☐

If the dumping of sewage continues even at its present rate,
Lake Monarch will be dead in ten years.

If the dumping of sewage con-tinues even at its present rate, Lake Monarch will be dead in ten years.

In identifying topic and key, we ignore the adverb clause we've just moved to the beginning. The topic is _____.
The key is _____. ☐

Lake Monarch
dead in ten years

We can now add statement D2 and have a final paragraph, but we will have missed the opportunity of giving our reader a few concrete ideas about what a dead Lake Monarch would be like.

If the dumping of sewage continues even at its present rate, Lake Monarch will be dead in ten years. **The algae will continue to multiply until they have taken over the lake entirely.** We can add this sentence because it (follows topic and key, adds information about part of the sentence before). ☐

follows topic and key

The algae will continue to multiply until they have taken over the lake entirely. **They will suffocate the few remaining fish.**
We can add this sentence because it (follows topic and key, adds information about part of the sentence before). ☐

adds information about part of the sentence before

The algae will continue to multiply until they have taken over the lake entirely. **They will suffocate the few remaining fish.**

Here we have still another clumsy sequence that we can improve by embedding the second sentence into the first. Use the *-ing* form of the verb to make a verb cluster:

suffocating the few remaining fish

The algae will continue to multiply until they have taken over the lake entirely, _____

_____ . □

If the dumping of sewage continues even at its present rate, Lake Monarch will be dead in ten years. . . . **The beaches will continue to collect waste chemicals and rotting organic matter.**

follows topic and key

We can add this sentence because it (follows topic and key, adds information about part of the sentence before). □

The beaches will continue to collect waste chemicals and rotting organic matter. **They will become nothing more than poisonous, reeking marshes.**

follows topic and key

We can add this sentence because it (follows topic and key, adds information about part of the sentence before). □

The beaches will continue to collect waste chemicals and rotting organic matter. **They will become nothing more than poisonous, reeking marshes.**

We can combine these sentences effectively by making the second into an adverb clause introduced by *until:*

until they become nothing more than poisonous, reeking marshes

The beaches will continue to collect waste chemicals and rotting organic matter _____

_____ . □

Finally, we can add statement D2 from our outline:

Lake Monarch can be saved and restored to health only if the cities upstream are forced by law to stop using the Blue River as a convenient sewer for their growing populations.

This sentence (follows topic and key, adds information about part of the sentence before). □

follows topic and key

For a look at the final paragraph, read the finished essay printed on pages 190–191. But first we need a title for our paper.

Effects of Algae and Other Degradants on Lake Monarch

A Lake is Dying

Lake Monarch Is Polluted

The Chemistry of Pollution in a Lake

Titles should be short, simple, striking. Which of these seems to fit the job? _____ □

A Lake Is Dying

A Lake Is Dying

Lake Monarch is dying. Until recently this large lake in the northwest corner of the state was pure and inviting, enjoyed by swimmers and fishermen from the time of the first settlers. Now, polluted by tons of raw sewage, it is rapidly becoming a foul-smelling cesspool, where wildlife sickens and where swimmers and fishermen venture at their risk.

Most of the sewage flows into Lake Monarch from the Blue River. The biggest source of the sewage is Crescent City, five miles upstream from the lake. The population of Crescent City has grown from 10,000 thirty years ago to the present 150,000, and its sewage has increased with the rising population. Now the city pumps partly treated sewage into the Blue River at the rate of fifty million gallons a day. In addition, five small towns farther upstream pump into the Blue River twenty million gallons of untreated sewage a day. Most of the sewage flowing into the lake settles there, each day's flood adding another wave of waste and poisons to the water and beaches.

In sewage, the chemicals that do the most damage to a lake are phosphorus from household detergents and nitrogen. Large quantities of these chemicals mean the rapid growth of algae, an extremely small form of plant life that turns healthy clear lake water into a muddy green. When algae die, they sink to the bottom and decay, using up the oxygen in the deep water necessary for the survival of fish. In Lake Monarch the proliferation of algae has strangled all but a few hardy survivors of the walleye, bass, perch, and whitefish that once abounded.

Along the shoreline, the once sandy beaches are becoming quagmires of mud and sewage. Pools of chemicals collect there, adding powerfully to the stench of rotting organic waste. Soggy paper, rusted cans, and broken milk cartons lie half-buried in the mud. Maggots, mosquitoes, and bloodworms multiply in the poisonous soup near shore, as well as bacteria such as *Salmonella*, which make the water unsafe even for swimming.

If the dumping of sewage continues even at its present rate, Lake Monarch will be dead in ten years. The algae will continue to multiply until they have taken over the lake entirely, suffocating the few remaining fish. The beaches will continue to collect waste chemicals and rotting organic matter until they become nothing more than piosonous, reeking marshes. Lake Monarch can be saved and restored to health only if the cities upstream are forced by law to stop using the Blue River as a convenient sewer for their growing populations.